KIM ██████

Horse
WISDOM

LIFE LESSONS FOR HUMANITY

Printed in the USA

First Edition

ISBN: 978-1-955346-13-9

Cover & Layout Design: Heather Dakota

Author photo by David Ramage

Photos:
pages 71, 87, 103 © Kim Hallin
pages 35, 125, 141 Pixabay
pages 7, 8, 15, 16, 26, 36, 43, 44, 52, 58, 64, 72, 80, 88, 95, 96, 104, 112, 120, 126, 132 stock.adobe.com

Wyrd & Wyld Publishing
Spokane, WA

Learn more at www.kimhallin.com

*This book is dedicated to Shoki, Markus,
and the sacred Circle of Horses.*

Praise for Horse Wisdom

"In a literary world where there are many books offered in a language that is only understood by those in the industry, this refreshing book shares the wisdom of the horse in bite sized pieces that are easily digestible, accessible to all, relatable, and transferable. Whether you are a seasoned horse person or someone who has only dreamed of being near a horse, Horse Wisdom: Life Lessons for Humanity has stories that you can understand and "nuggets" of profound wisdom to apply to your own life." – **Lynda Watson**, Equine Leadership magazine

"Horse Wisdom: Life Lessons for Humanity is a wonderful, eye-opening book! It's powerful, yet gentle. Beginning with the first chapter, Kim shows that she is a humble human learning from horses and sharing her personal journey, not an expert "lecturing." This is an important book that is touching and readable! You'll return to these pages again and again." – **Michael Gordon**, Ross School of Business, University of Michigan

"Living in a world of distraction and disconnection has left many of us feeling lost. We've easily become consumed by the external world and forgotten what really matters. This beautiful book and its teachings remind us to wake up to what's present in our lives—to connect with ourselves and others around us. Through the wisdom of horses, we are given the gift of remembering to reconnect and communicate through our heart, rather than our mind. When we drop our egos and allow ourselves to open our hearts and minds, we're given the gift of "seeing" things differently. Kim Hallin's book is a reminder that we have a choice as to how we relate to our world." – **Bonnie Compton**, author of Mothering With Courage

"Horse Wisdom: Life Lessons for Humanity *is a hugely helpful book for ALL horse owners, riders, and equestrians in regard to viewing and treating horses with more compassion. The book is also a beautiful reminder, backed up by facts and science, of how disconnected humanity has become from the rest of the natural world. I loved how this message was carried throughout the book in a gentle and non-judgmental way. I especially appreciated Kim's bent toward ethology and evolutionary biology and heritage, for both humans and equines!"*
– **Angela Dunning**, author of *The Horse Leads the Way: Honoring the True Role of the Horse in Equine Facilitated Practice*

"Kim Hallin's story of her experience and observations with horses and nature is a timely recognition and urgent message for humanity to wake-up and remember our inherent connection to our planet and our sensory abilities to feel and know the truth. Only then can we shift our societal anxieties based on perpetual misinformation to solutions and behavior that are actually in our best interest."
– **Schelli Whitehouse**, author of *The Business of Coaching with Horses*

"Kim Hallin has a gift, and she's shared it with all of us through Horse Wisdom: Life Lessons for Humanity. *Once you start to unwrap the lessons in this book, and the more layers you expose, the deeper the treasures. Whether or not you have equine experience, Kim and the horses have something we desperately need, and yet, have had all along. For those in the horse world, liberate yourselves from any preconceived training, use this book to restart your journey, and follow the horses' lead. See where they take you. And then, share the gift of horse wisdom with those without access to these great teachers."* – **Nancy Muñoz**, FreeHorse Arts

KIM HALLIN

Table of Contents

Introduction to Horse Wisdom

When receiving horse wisdom it's easy to say, "That's all well and good, but it can't be applied in the human world." Precisely. If it could, it would be human-oriented wisdom. We already have plenty of that. Embracing horse wisdom requires a willingness to look beyond what humanity believes about itself. Embodying horse wisdom requires stepping away from the trappings of human life as we know it. "Why throw the baby out with the bath water?" some might ask. But what if humanity threw the baby out a long time ago, and now, we're wading around in a tub of tepid, murky water?

The struggle to imagine how humanity can disentangle ourselves from the harnesses of our own making is real. Unbridling an angry beast is a delicate process. The human species has become fixated on the idea of *fixing*. We see ourselves as both the fixers and the species that needs fixing. Horse wisdom reminds us there's a better way. Transformation starts when we release our attachment to all that's no longer serving us. Horses know that the world isn't broken, and neither are we. This book is an invitation to remember that for yourself.

But what exactly *is* horse wisdom?

During the tumultuous spring and summer of 2020, I sought solace with my horses. Due to the Covid-19 lock down, I was forced to spend weeks alone on my farm. I carried my folding chair out to the horses' pasture each morning to spend time in their world, soaking in the soothing sights and sounds of nature. Being with the herd felt like a salve. Their calm, peaceful presence helped me release my attachment to the chaos permeating the human world. Soon, I craved my morning meditations with the herd. The horses seemed to enjoy our meditative time together, too. I regularly spend time outside on my farm, interacting with the horses and facilitating equine-assisted learning experiences for the public. This was different. I realized how easy it is to be with the horses without actually being *with them.*

When I work with clients, it's inevitable (and appropriate) that we carry our mental and emotional ties to the human world into the pasture. Now, I came into the pasture specifically to leave the human world behind. The horses were utterly unaffected by the stress that was taking the domestic world by storm. Their grounded energy felt primal. I marveled at how the herd stayed centered despite living a life of captivity. I wanted to know how it felt to be in their skin. I gave my child's mind permission to imagine I was one of the herd. The grass pricked my lips as I grazed. I savored the aromatic smells emanating from the plants and Earth beneath my nose. The warm sun felt comforting on my back while the breeze blew gently through my mane. The tips of my tail hairs tickled my lower legs, keeping the insects at bay. The rhythmic sounds of my herd mates grazing as the birds above us called, then counter-called reassuringly, filled my heart with a deep knowing that all was well in the world.

Being present and grounded requires an intentional honoring of what's actually available—right here, right now.

Nothing more. Nothing less. An ancient knowing deep in my bones whispered, "This is the meaning of life." And then, a message from the horses dropped in:

> "We can help you separate your understanding of life from everything the human world has taught you to believe. Life existed—and has been thriving—since long before human thinking took the reins. The natural world remains unadulterated in its way of being and always will. You, too, are part of this natural world. Human thoughts and beliefs keep your species stuck on a path of isolation and despair. These struggles are of your own making. You will take other species out with you, but the natural world will survive. It's resilient by design. Humanity's story doesn't have to end the way it's headed. If you let us, we're here to guide you home."

Since that day, I see everything differently. Our preoccupation with all that's exclusively human disconnects us from what's brilliantly universal. Through this new lens, a world that formerly seemed dismal, complicated, and impossible to navigate, suddenly looks vivid, simple, and clear. I can feel horse wisdom affirming me. "Yessssss," it says. "The true meaning of life is unrelated to human-focused goals, agendas, beliefs, philosophies, religions, political systems, governments, jobs, and economic goals. No other life form concerns itself with your human distractions."

I don't so much hear these words as I feel them with a deep, ancestral inner-knowing. That knowing is what called me to write this book. The writing itself took me on a journey of re-membering what life is like for the rest of life on Earth. Humanity doesn't have to stay in the place of separateness we created. We've lingered here too long already or maybe not quite long enough. The horses keep assuring me that awareness takes the time it takes. They're masters at being patient and also eager to guide us back to living in balance with all life.

How to Use This Book

When it comes to receiving and embodying horse wisdom, there are no rules. Take your time with this book and the lessons from the horses. Lift what you can from the pages. Allow the words to help you explore the depths of your inner-knowing and wonder. The lessons will walk you through some personally profound experiences with horses. Each lesson ends with a few of my favorite takeaways. I'll also introduce you to the equine sages, past and present, who continue to bless my life. All were with me as I wrote, re-wrote, edited, and re-edited. As the saying goes, "They approve these messages," as a launching point for further discussion. Beginning with the end in mind requires holding space for what's to come.

In order to remain focused on the over-arching lessons, I have chosen to refer to all members of the human species collectively using the terms "humans" or "humanity." In some cases, I distinguish between modern humans and our more primitive ancestors. Likewise, I have intentionally chosen to refer to the equine collective as "horses," distinguishing occasionally between horses living in the wild and horses living domestically. I recognize and deeply honor the unique journeys, experiences, and perspectives of every living individual (human, equine, and otherwise) as well as the varied beliefs and traditions held by humans from different cultures and backgrounds. The reality of today's world is that we, to some extent, live at the mercy of the pervasive human mindset in the western world.

Let's start at the beginning with the end in mind. The lessons in this book are designed to be progressive and cumulative, so jump to a topic that calls to you. Each lesson was written to stand alone. As you read, lean into the feelings and questions that arise inside you. Notice when my words bump against the edges of your comfort zone. When the words touch the voice of your soul, echoing something it's been longing to say or hear, celebrate this knowing. Pay attention to the bulleted takeaways at the end of each lesson. Do they resonate? What else could you add? Horses remind us that life is meant to be a collaborative, embodied experience.

We shouldn't try to think, write, or read our way through our experiences in isolation. In order to embody the lessons of horse wisdom, the horses and I encourage you to journal and talk with your friends, family members, pets, and co-workers about these topics. How can you play with applying horse wisdom in your life? If you find yourself wanting to explore this question more deeply, I've included journal prompts and other resources, see page 150.

We're all in this together.

May HORSE WISDOM guide us home.

LESSON ONE

∞

You're Free to Define Freedom for Yourself

Horses are uniquely positioned to help humanity re-evaluate our perceptions around the meaning of freedom. Unlike their free-roaming ancestors, domestic horses live a life of captivity. However, they are rarely motivated to escape. Most horses could easily jump or break down the fences that we use to keep them corralled. They could run for freedom, but they don't. In the rare instances when domestic horses get loose, what they seek bears little resemblance to humanity's concept of freedom.

Many years ago, my neighbor's horses got loose in the middle of the night. The commotion outside woke me up. My first thought was that my own horses had somehow gotten loose. I jumped out of bed, grabbed my flashlight, and scurried out the door. As I rounded the corner of the house, I quickly made out the silhouettes of my three horses—all safely inside their fenced enclosure. I could also make out the shapes of four horses grazing on the opposite side of the fence. A fifth loose horse was standing a little farther down the fenceline, sniffing noses with my herd elder over the top rail.

I realized the loose horses belonged to my neighbor. In my rush, I forgot to grab my cell phone. I didn't want to risk losing sight of the horses should they head down the road in one direction or the other, so I grabbed a halter, lead line, and handful of treats from the nearby shed. My plan was to entice at least one of the horses into letting me approach so I could put the halter on. My neighbor's horses were tightly bonded to one another. If I took one member of the herd back home, the others would likely follow.

Things didn't go as planned.

The horses looked my way as I approached, but as soon as they saw the halter and leadrope, they turned the other way. As I watched all five horses trot away, a fleeting sense of panic washed over me. If there's one thing you can count on with herd animals, it's that they'll always stick together! I knew chasing after the horses would ignite their prey animal flight response, so I willed myself to stay where I was. I held my breath and watched. What happened next surprised me. Instead of taking off down the street (as I feared), the horses headed straight back to their owner's front yard and quietly settled into grazing again.

Meanwhile, my horses got distressed as soon as the visiting herd left. Fascination crept in as I watched this all unfold. The panic I'd been feeling faded away. My neighbor's horses clearly didn't want to be caught, but they also had no interest in running away. My human brain tried to rationalize their decision. "They must want to stay close to home," I thought. Familiar territory. Even as this thought passed, my gut told me there was something more going on. If the horses wanted to stay close to home, why did they leave in the first place? As if on cue, my herd elder, Shoki, let out an anxious whinny, which was answered immediately by a reassuring nicker from across the street. "Don't worry, we're still here," the neighboring horse seemed to say. And then it dawned on me, the horses wanted to be together. All of them.

As herd animals, horses value community above all else. They have no use for the concept of property lines. It makes no sense to horses why we choose to keep some of them separated from others using fences. My neighbor's and my herd have lived across the street from one another for many years. There's a great deal of familiarity between the two herds, yet the horses rarely have the opportunity to interact face-to-face. All they wanted was to spend time together as a united herd.

Still, I had a conundrum. How was I going to get my neighbor's horses safely secured inside their fence again? I worked with the momentum of the moment by herding the horses down my neighbor's driveway toward their pasture gate, which I could see was open. Clearly that's how they escaped! However, my new strategy didn't work any better than the first one. As soon as I exerted a bit of herding energy, the horse closest to me split off and headed straight back across the street to my farm. Within seconds, the other four darted past me, too. Irritation set in. I thought about knocking on my neighbor's door, but I was still somewhat worried the horses might run off if left unattended.

My horses were overjoyed by the return of the neighboring herd. They pranced along the fenceline, nickering their excitement. One thing was crystal clear, my neighbor's escapees were no more interested in returning to their pasture than they were in running away.

Members of wild horse herds know and recognize one another because the horses share grazing lands and frequently meet at the local watering hole. As I witnessed the instinctual equine drive to gather unfolding before my eyes, I appreciated horse priorities on a deeper level. I also realized that all I had to do to recapture the escapees was think like a horse!

When I put myself in their hooves, the solution became obvious. The best way to catch the escapees was to invite them onto my property. I crossed the street and opened the gate at the top of my driveway. Then, I allowed my neighbor's horses to follow me in. As soon as I opened the gate, they cooperated as if this had been their plan all along, voluntarily re-capturing themselves on my property. Within seconds, all the horses were happily commiserating over the internal paddock fence that still separated my horses from my neighbor's horses. Feeling quite satisfied with myself, I went inside and called my neighbor who laughed upon hearing about the antics that had gone on while she slept.

She came over, and we easily haltered the horses and led them home. The horses seemed to understand that there was no point in resisting. For the next couple of days, members of both herds continued to call to one another periodically. After having the opportunity to unite face-to-face, even briefly, the two herds connected energetically.

My neighbor's horses hadn't intentionally planned their late-night escape. They took advantage of an opportunity when the gate was left unlatched. As long as their basic needs are met, horses don't spend their days lamenting about being confined. In fact, many domestic horses appreciate the safety of fences that keep predators and unfamiliar activities at a distance.

For humans, the word freedom in relation to horses typically conjures images of stampeding herds galloping across the plains. This fantasy fails to acknowledge that wild horses only stampede when they feel threatened. The freedom horses value most is not the freedom to run unobstructed. It's the freedom to form communities and nurture friendships that help them feel safe.

Humans consider any type of confinement or imprisonment to be a violation of freedom. But, horses can feel free as long as they have the liberty to behave according to their innate nature as communal herd animals. This includes building relationships and being free to engage in species-specific activities such as grazing and foraging. If humanity thought about freedom in terms of the ability to express our innate nature as *Homo sapiens*, how might our concepts of freedom shift? Do we even know what freedom means to us?

In the early years of human existence, our species lived as nomadic hunter-gatherers relying heavily on our innate evolutionary gifts, instincts, and the natural world to survive. Although we now consider our early ancestors uncivilized, they likely felt far more free than we do today.

The individual and collective behaviors of civilized humans are largely directed by cultural expectations and rules of law. Human-constructed systems set limits on behavior and are inflexible, constraining, and unfair because the consequences for violating established codes can't be readily individualized or contextualized.

Mother Nature has a far superior approach. In a wild horse herd, each individual horse makes choices and adjusts behavior based on personal or collective consequences. It's not specific acts of behavior that are seen as problematic, but the impact one's behaviors and choices have within the larger herd community. Within this framework, individual freedom—for all species—is possible because authentic personalized consequences ensure long-term order and balance for the entire planet.

As an example, wild horses intentionally choose their living companions and communities based on the shared experience of living together. Within a larger herd community (potentially hundreds of horses), various long-term *family bands* naturally develop. A family band is a voluntary (or organic) grouping of horses, ranging in size from a single bonded pair to a dozen or more horses who choose to live together. Most horse bands fall into one of two categories: *natal bands* and *bachelor bands*. Natal bands focus around the work of child rearing. Friendships of brotherhood define the bachelor bands. The members support one another in developing effective parenting and mentoring skills for the future success of the herd. Very deep, lifelong friendships develop within these family units but the individuals don't necessarily live together for life. By two to three years of age, youngsters leave their natal band. A variety of environmental or predatory situations can cause mature horses to reorganize their living situations as well.

Within an established herd or band community, individual relationships are nurtured through authenticity. These relationships are managed through honest communication and respect for personal boundaries. The collective desire to maintain peaceful relations within a herd community is driven by a deep understanding that isolated living comes with a significantly higher risk of succumbing to predation (i.e. death). It also results in a much less fulfilling life experience. In all cases, personal consequences, whether subtle or extreme, govern horse behavior and choices.

As humanity separates from the flexibility of a natural form of freedom, the less free we feel. When we rely too heavily on external systems of control, we lose touch with our innate ability to embrace personal consequences as the natural mechanism for governing behavior and choices.

Horse wisdom reminds us:

- We all have the power to define our personal and collective freedom.
- Freedom from consequences invites chaos and creates dependence on unnaturally rigid rules and laws.
- Captivity is not necessarily the antithesis of feeling free.

LESSON TWO

❧

Ownership is Unnatural

Ownership is a purely human concept that doesn't exist in nature. Wild horses and other undomesticated animals engage in a more natural approach to managing competition for vital resources: territoriality. The natural attachment to, and organically driven defense of, specific territories is an instinctual strategy for reducing competition within balanced ecosystems. Overlapping species-specific territories ensure adequate access to shared resources including food, water, and shelter.

Ownership is a different beast. Black's Law Dictionary defines ownership as "the complete dominion, title, or proprietary right in a thing or claim." Ownership gives individuals of the human species (or legally recognized groups of humans) *legally enforceable rights* to control the things we own, including the economic benefits. In contrast to the flexible and interdependent nature of territoriality, ownership as a system is exclusive, inflexible, and oppressive.

Humanity hasn't always operated under the influence of ownership. When our distant ancestors lived in balance with one another, the animal kingdom, and the land, we honored, and participated in, the natural practice of territoriality. It's hard to determine exactly why or how humanity shifted toward systems of ownership as the basis for our society. This led to the birth of many other purely human concepts including money, assets, debt, private property, and even war. These concepts evolved into today's well-established global economic and social systems. Systems that are inherently oppressive, not just for us, but for all life on Earth.

Now, humanity is stuck in the grip of what could be described as a self-perpetuating form of "forced addiction" to ownership. Our society requires us to work jobs so we can receive money to buy things, which we then own. Participating in this system of ownership feels good initially. Before long the temporary "high" of becoming an owner (i.e. feelings of independence, accomplishment, power, control, responsibility, and even stewardship) wears off. That's when the harsh reality of *being owned by the things we own* sets in. The oppressive nature of ownership increases exponentially when what we own is another living being. My experiences as a horse owner have helped me understand the trappings of systemic ownership at a deep level. The horse industry is a microcosm that provides powerful insight into the larger cycles at play in ownership-based systems.

Lilith

Lilith was the first horse I owned. My husband purchased her as a 30th birthday gift, but I had fallen in love with her months earlier. Lilith was the kindest, steadiest, least complicated horse at the barn where I rode. After a horrible riding accident in college, she helped me regain my confidence. I felt safe with Lilith.

In the beginning, owning Lilith felt exhilarating. Being a horse owner granted me permission to come to the barn any-time to brush Lilith's beautiful bay coat, gaze wonder-fully into her soulful brown eyes, or sit quietly under a tree watching her graze in the summer sun. Ownership gave me the sole authority to make decisions on Lilith's behalf and to do whatever I chose to do with her (within legal limits). Or so I thought.

Anyone who has boarded their horse at a barn facility owned by someone else understands there is a hierarchy inherent in ownership. In most cases, property ownership trumps horse ownership. In order to gain full legal authority to make ALL management decisions related to the horse I now owned, I had to buy my own farm.

It doesn't take long for new horse owners to crash from the initial high of horse ownership. Being responsible for the physical, mental, and emotional well-being of a thousand-pound prey animal, (and quite possibly a farm property on top of that), is incredibly stressful and expensive.

At minimum, horses eat two to three percent of their body weight in hay and forage per day and produce 50 to 60 pounds of manure every day. It's quite challenging to keep their bodies balanced nutritionally if they don't have the freedom to graze at will on a varied diet of grasses, weeds, leaves, berries, nuts, flowers, and twigs for up to 18 hours a day. This requires a very large property. Horses also need a lot of space so their bodies can stay in constant gentle movement. They're happiest when living in the company and safety of a trusted herd community.

Most humans are ill-equipped to serve as effective custodians for our equine charges. However, our desire to have horses in our lives compels us to engage in horse ownership despite these immense challenges. Gone are the days when horses and humans shared naturally overlapping organic territories that allowed us to live in harmony with one another without the complications of ownership.

After owning Lilith for six years and my husband and I fell on hard times, I made the heartbreaking decision to sell her.

The ownership paradigm convinced us that *essential* assets such as houses and cars are more valuable than relationships with (or responsibility to) the animals we own, particularly when it comes to horses and other livestock. While horses are often loved as dearly as dogs and cats, in many countries, horses are legally designated as livestock rather than companion animals. The horse industry has lobbied hard to maintain this legal designation, which allows horses to be used as beasts of burden, sport, and hobby.

Horses are expensive to purchase and maintain, humanity believes that it's *fair and just* to expect or require horses to "earn their keep." This attitude toward horses has long been normalized in human society, but it creates an ethical dilemma no horse owner wants to admit. If horses were dogs or cats, most of us would be guilty of animal cruelty for how we treat and use them. If horses were people, the vast majority would be considered indentured servants.

While the truth about humanity's relationship to horses is disturbing, the facts don't make horse owners bad people. In fact, all the horse owners I know love their horses with all their hearts. We've been conditioned to think and behave the way our ownership-based systems require. We suffer serious emotional consequences as a result, namely guilt and shame.

After I sold Lilith, I couldn't shake the feelings of guilt. Six months after Lili left us, I received word that she had broken her leg while playing in the pasture. Her new owner had no choice but to euthanize her. My legal responsibility for Lilith's well-being ended the moment I signed her bill of sale, but my conscience still felt responsible. Even though her death was a no-fault accident, I knew that my selfish choice had landed her in the wrong place at the wrong time. Ownership systems are oppressive, because they compel us to make choices that are out of alignment with our hearts, which can lead to unnecessary pain and suffering.

Tempo & Puck

When it comes to the hard truth about ownership, my second wake-up call came in the form of a headstrong mare named Tempo. I became Tempo's owner at the time of her birth by owning her mother (Puck). The laws of horse ownership dictate that the owner of a foal's mother at the time of foaling, also owns the foal. I decided to breed Puck because I wanted the opportunity to mold a young horse into exactly what I wanted her to be. The mindset of ownership creates feelings of power and control that lead to a belief that we have the right to control things no one should have dominion over, including another living being's life.

At the age of one year, Tempo was diagnosed with a developmental bone disorder. My vision of molding her into a competitive steed was shattered before she could even be started under saddle. When several surgeons reviewed her scans, the situation became even more devastating. Tempo was given a very low prognosis for being able to heal enough to live out her life comfortably as a non-ridden companion animal.

Suddenly, I found myself faced with an unexpected life-or-death decision on behalf of a young horse I loved and whose life I had a hand in creating. It felt like an impossible situation, and no one, not even the veterinarians, were willing to advise me about what decision to make. They laid out my treatment options, provided detailed information about possible complications, and shared the rather dismal success rates for horses with similar diagnoses. How could I possibly base a life-or-death decision for Tempo on hypothetical scenarios?

Desperate for guidance, I turned to Tempo for help. After

all, it was *her* life and no ownership papers could change that fact. Moments of awakening shift our perspective and create a sense of clarity in the midst of confusion or despair. Even though Tempo was experiencing physical pain, nothing about her demeanor, mindset, or attitude suggested she was giving up. Her will to live was strong and unwavering.

As soon as I stopped to consider Tempo's feelings and experiences, it was obvious that there was no need to make a life-or-death decision. Relieved of that burden, I turned my full attention to making treatment decisions. It was a step in the right direction, but I was still caught in the ownership snare of making life-altering decisions on behalf of another living being (who was not my child).

During her extended treatment and rehabilitation over the next eight months, I struggled and consistently failed to find creative ways to keep Tempo sane. This period marked one of the darkest chapters in my journey of horse ownership. I often felt trapped between a veterinarian's recommendation and what I believed was best for Tempo's long-term physical and emotional prognosis. Keeping her confined meant she was missing critical aspects of herd socialization during a key phase in equine development. As Tempo's owner, I feared for her future in a human world where horses are valued primarily as commodities and beasts of burden. Not a day passed when I didn't question whether I was making the right decisions.

As prey animals (meaning that in nature they are hunted and killed by other animals), horses evolved to rely on flight as their primary line of defense when stressed, confused, or afraid. Tempo didn't understand *why* I was making the choices I made, but she recognized me as the "all powerful one" who controlled the door to a stall. Tempo's free-wheeling early childhood had not prepared her to cope with the sudden shift to life inside a prison cell. Isolated, confined, and confused, she had only one thing on her mind—escape.

Each time I refused to let Tempo exit, she grew more frustrated and resentful. When I entered her stall, Tempo behaved aggressively. She knew my entrance preceded the administration of daily medications and other treatment protocols. I wanted to spend more time with Tempo that was enjoyable, but the reality of horse ownership left me between a rock and hard place. I had to pick up additional paid work to cover the costs of Tempo's veterinary care and medications.

Meanwhile, the internal switch that controlled which primal coping strategy Tempo needed to call on flipped from flight to fight. Watching a horse I loved struggle to cope with her lost autonomy was torture for me. Nothing I tried helped her make peace with what I needed to do (as her owner) to support her physical healing. As a result of my inability to provide Tempo with what she needed to cope, she made it her mission to ensure my experience was every bit as painful (physically and emotionally) as her's.

Eventually, Tempo's body made an amazing recovery. Today, she lives an active, happy life on my farm, frolicking freely without indication of pain. However, Tempo continues to be a horse who refuses to bear the brunt of unhealthy thought and behavior patterns born out of the human mindset of ownership and control.

She's taught me (the hard way) how to interpret subtle equine body language and what it means to relate to a horse in a way that honors the horse's feelings. This makes Tempo a horse few people would find enjoyable to own.

Sometimes I wonder how different she would be if I hadn't forced her to endure the recommended treatment protocols. Would her body have recovered on its own? Would she be living a life of chronic pain? Would she feel less guarded toward humans about our intentions? Of course, there's no way to answer any of these questions with certainty. The stars simply aligned the way they needed to and created a perfect storm of intervention that landed both of us in a powerful position to share our story. The ripple effect may spawn new moments of awareness, intervention, and clarity for others who struggle within our human systems of ownership.

My experiences with Tempo dug me even deeper into the depths of horse ownership. This horse is neither physically or emotionally suited for use (or resale) in the horse industry. I've made a commitment to owning Tempo (and her beloved herd mates) for life. This means making provisions for the horses as part of my estate planning (yet another ownership-based burden we carry). Even as I continue to participate actively in the systems of ownership, I no longer buy into the false narrative that ownership (of any kind) is something we should aspire to or take pride in.

As custodian and caretaker of horses, my role provides an opportunity to better understand the pitfalls inherent in ownership of other living beings. I also practice empathy as a means of mitigating the unhealthy power and control that ownership gives me over my horses.

Andy, Shoki, Markus, and Relicario

There are four other horses I've walked in ownership with. You'll meet them as the lessons in this book unfold. Collectively the members of my herd helped me understand how humanity can find ways out from under the oppressive cycles of ownership. The task seems almost insurmountable.

However, Tempo handed me the key: *free will*. We may be

trapped within a system of ownership, but that doesn't mean we have to believe it is healthy.

We can begin to make choices, large and small, that loosen the grip systemic ownership has on our lives. We can point out the truth rather than perpetuating misbeliefs. We can look to the natural world for healthier approaches to living in a balanced, sustainable community. Humanity can and will evolve past our current obsession with ownership, emerging as a wiser, more compassionate species on the other side. We deserve to do it for ourselves, the horses, and the planet.

Horse wisdom reminds us:

- Ownership provides a powerful opportunity to explore, experience, and understand the nature of oppressive systems.
- Ownership has become a human addiction.
- Humanity created ownership. Only we have the power to end it.
- Systems of ownership must evolve to allow for free-will, especially when owning horses or other livestock.

LESSON THREE

Mind the Stories You Tell

*E*very horse, like every human, has a story. The difference is that horses don't define or label themselves, one another, or humans based on past experiences or situations. Horses, like humans, can carry trauma and triggers related to past experiences, or develop unhealthy coping strategies to deal with stress. However, horses actively look for opportunities to heal and work to release emotional baggage that is no longer serving them. Horses are good at responding and adapting to whatever happens, freely becoming whoever they need to be in the present moment. Humans pass judgment on one another and ourselves for how we respond to the experiences we encounter. We use labels to define who we are and tell stories to explain or defend our behaviors and choices. We attempt to use labels to clarify without acknowledging the ways these labels limit us. Horses can model and remind us how to adapt to environmental and situational changes and evolve into whatever the moment calls for.

Shortly after launching my equine-assisted learning (EAL) business, a friend connected me with a local BodyTalk™ practitioner, named Jana Brady, who was looking for an opportunity to interact with horses. Jana explained that she conducted a session with one of her clients in an unusual location: a horse farm. The session took place outside the fence enclosing one of the pastures. "About half-way into the session, a horse walked up and started reaching his nose over the fence to show me exactly where this woman's body needed attention!" Jana exclaimed. She described how the horse pointed his muzzle to the areas that needed attention, right before she was about to move her hands there. "The horse sensed the same things I did!" Jana marveled. The experience was so profound, she hoped to find a herd of horses on private property, versus at a public boarding facility, where she could explore the dynamic further.

Intrigued but confused, I asked Jana to clarify what BodyTalk™ was. She explained that BodyTalk™ professionals utilize the innate wisdom of the body to support self-healing, particularly to recover from injury or illness. My mind immediately jumped to Tempo who had suffered a developmental bone disorder as a yearling and was struggling to bounce back from the physical and emotional ramifications of extended stall confinement during her recovery. From a veterinary perspective, Tempo's injury was fully healed. But I sensed that she still felt stiff and ill-at-ease in her body much of the time. I wondered if BodyTalk™ could help her.

"Can you do BodyTalk™ on a horse?" I asked. "Yes," Jana replied, "BodyTalk is supportive for any body! I've already done some work with dogs and cats. When I'm supporting an animal it's most effective (and less invasive) to use the owner as a conduit."

"What does that mean?" I asked. Jana explained that as long as the horse is a willing participant and open to talking to her intuitively, she could register the horse's answers to her "yes" or "no" questions through the level of resistance she felt when gently moving my wrist. I'm sure my expression spoke for itself. "I don't understand," I said. "How is that even possible?"

"Animals are intimately connected with their human

custodians on an energetic level," Jana explained. "And they intuitively understand how the BodyTalk™ process works. We can even work with your horses from outside the fence. I'll stand beside you and ask you to relax the muscles in your arm and hand. Then, I'll monitor the tension in your wrist to confirm answers when I ask clarifying questions to the horses. You won't know when I'm asking questions because I'll do it intuitively. Your body will simply serve as a conduit."

I looked at Jana in disbelief.

"Our bodies already know how to engage in this energetic conversation," she assured me. "It may sound impossible to you, but animals don't overthink it. They exist in a realm of energy exchange. You don't need to understand how it works, but I hope you'll remain open-minded and give it a chance."

My rational brain told me this was craziness, but Jana was spoken of so highly, as a person and practitioner. What did I have to lose? She offered to come to my farm for free to practice BodyTalk™ in exchange for a safe place to explore healing in partnership with horses. Jana wouldn't lay hands on my horses, so there was no way she could physically harm them. The only thing giving me pause was my preconceived notions or the stories in my head. I agreed that Jana could come out for a test run.

When she arrived a few days later, this session didn't go the way we thought it would. As it turned out, Tempo was not on-board. BodyTalk™ practitioners start by asking intuitively for the subject's permission to proceed and engage in conversation. My opinionated mare's response was immediate and decisive. I'd been watching Tempo, but I didn't see her bat an eye. It was Jana's words that caught my attention. "You have a sassy one there!" she chided. Her words couldn't have been more true. How did Jana know this about Tempo? The horse hadn't even looked in our direction. "Your horse essentially told me to go to hell," the practitioner laughed.

This woman had never met my horses, she claimed to know almost nothing about horses, yet somehow she attributed a response to Tempo that fit the mare's personality to a T. Tempo can be extremely testy, particularly with people she doesn't know. If Tempo feels vulnerable or put-upon, she becomes defensive.

I was dumbfounded. "Did Tempo literally tell you to go to hell? I mean, you actually heard her say those words?"

"No, I didn't hear the words," Jana responded. "I felt them." She went on to explain that when she communicates with animals their messages come through in a variety of ways. Sometimes she receives energetic sensations, sometimes she sees colors, other times the communication comes in the form of symbols or occasionally as fully developed thoughts or concepts that pop into her head out of nowhere.

I'd been warned many times (by people whose opinions I trusted) not to believe in woo-woo stuff like animal communication. "*Those people* make stuff up or tell you things that could be true for anyone!" Several friends told me stories of being swindled by so-called animal communicators. Hearing this practitioner tell me that my horse wouldn't give permission to be communicated with seemed like, perhaps, an easy out. I decided to take it.

"If Tempo isn't a willing partner, we can't do this, right?"

"Well, I always honor an animal's feelings and wouldn't try to engage without permission," Jana affirmed. "But, I could still put out an open invitation to see if any of the other horses want to participate." At this point, my curiosity got the better of me. "Sure," I said, "let's try that." I shared the names of the other horses with her. Within seconds of putting the question out to them, Jana exclaimed, "Shoki is volunteering! He seems very eager."

What transpired over the next hour was life-changing for me. Not only did I experience for myself how BodyTalk™ is facilitated, I gained incredible insights into the nature of healing and the profound wisdom of horses. Jana spoke, in intimate detail, of an event in Shoki's life that had occurred ten years prior. No one except me, Shoki, and the emergency veterinarian on call that night knew anything of the events. Shoki shared mental images portraying the treatment he'd received during an after-hours vet call for emergency colic. Jana had no idea about equine colic or how it's treated, and yet, she described the process in detail. This invasive procedure is standard protocol for treating colic in horses, particularly when an impaction is suspected. While clearly uncomfortable and often disconcerting for the horse, the procedure rarely causes complications.

My mind raced back to that horrible night. The young veterinarian arrived around 9:00PM and was not my normal vet. She introduced herself as a new addition to the clinic's team. In an emergency situation, horse owners can't be choosy about which on-call veterinarian shows up. Colic can quickly take a fatal turn. The young veterinarian took Shoki's vitals and palpated him rectally to confirm that he did, indeed, have a "minor" impaction. She wanted to tube him in order to lubricate his intestines with mineral oil. But the process didn't go smoothly. The young veterinarian had a difficult time getting the tube down Shoki's esophagus. I watched as my heavily sedated horse tilted his head and shuffled his feet, trying desperately to seek relief from the pain and discomfort.

In the end, the veterinarian pushed very hard to get the tube to go down. When it finally did, a stream of blood gushed out of Shoki's nose. I gasped, "Oh my goodness."

I'd witnessed a number of tubings previously, and there hadn't been any blood. The young veterinarian remained calm. "It's no big deal. It happens sometimes. The bleeding will stop soon," she assured me. I was scared, but she was right. The bleeding was short lived. Both of us quickly turned our attention to the urgent matter of getting the mineral oil into Shoki's stomach. Until Jana spoke of this incident, I had put the memory out of my mind.

Why was Shoki bringing this incident up now?

Jana explained that Shoki was showing her some scarring in his esophagus. When she asked him if the scarring was causing him pain or discomfort, I was pleased to hear his response was *no*. In fact, he said the scarring wasn't problematic at all. It served as a memory of the trauma he experienced that night. Shoki wanted me to be aware of this trauma because I was the only person who would understand what he had gone through.

"I feel horrible that he has scarring from that treatment," I lamented. "I knew the blood meant something but I dismissed it because the veterinarian dismissed it."

"Shoki isn't looking for an apology," Jana assured me. "He wanted you to know. Sometimes in order to heal from past trauma, we need our experience of the trauma to be seen and understood." My chest tightened and my eyes burned. Tears rolled down my cheek. I locked eyes with Shoki. That night had been traumatic for me, too. Now my fears and feelings were being brought to light and acknowledged. It felt good to let those harbored feelings rise to the surface and be released. Shoki sighed, lowered his head, and approached the fence. He lifted his face to meet mine and softly leaned his nostril against my cheek. His whiskers tickled my skin. The warmth of his breath enveloped me in a loving embrace of friendship.

"Healing isn't just a physical act," Jana explained.

"Sometimes our emotional scars run the deepest." After Shoki and I had our moment together, she performed some gentle tapping techniques to activate the chakras and help clear any lingering toxic energies stored deep within our bodies for so many years. Then, Jana asked Shoki if there was anything else he wanted to share.

"Shoki is encouraging you to mind the stories you tell," Jana said.

"What does he mean?" I asked.

"For example, he doesn't like it when you tell the story of his past and mention the name they used to call him. He doesn't feel the way you tell that story honors who he is."

It was another gut punch. I'd been telling Shoki's story for years. I explained about his rough early life, and how he'd been given the name *Insha'allah* because his handlers believed a rider could only stay on him if God willed it. My friend, Billie saved him, changed his name, and showered him with love and compassion. The story reflected on Shoki's damage. When he came to live with me, he was over reactive, spooky, and timid. The way I told Shoki's story, Billie and I were the heroes. She saved him. I helped him overcome his fears. The story wasn't *inaccurate*. But the primary motivation behind my telling of Shoki's story in that particular way was human ego. For the first time, I realized Shoki's story was hijacked and used for my purposes. Shoki is the hero of his own story. None of us should assume we know how someone else wants their story told, nor should we label in ways that limit who someone is. This includes beings of any species.

All of my horses, Shoki included, have demonstrated time and again that they're capable of becoming whoever they need to be in any given moment or situation. A horse's relationship with humans is only a small aspect of who they are. That day, as I thought about what I actually knew to be true about Shoki, what stood out was his monumental role and place of respect in my herd. My heart swelled with pride, not for my role in supporting his journey, but for his resiliency, spirit, and capacity to overcome. Most of all, I was grateful for the way my horses refuse to allow any one chapter of their stories to define who they are capable of becoming.

As I stood contemplating the depth of Shoki's profound message, Jana advised me that Shoki wasn't quite done. He had one more piece of wisdom to share: "Shoki says you should mind the other stories you tell as well, including the stories you tell yourself." I immediately thought of the negative self-talk that too often causes me to question my own potential or worth.

My experiences that day transformed the way I view my horses. They also changed the way I think about myself, my life, the way I relate to others, and my ability to honor and embrace the mysterious and unknown.

Horse wisdom reminds us:

- Stories are informative but should never definitively define someone.
- Labels are limiting. Use them with care.
- Shared experiences help us feel seen and understood.
- The story of human superiority limits the potential of humanity.
- The best answer to the question, "Who are you?" is "I am me."

LESSON FOUR

❧

Trust Yourself First

$\mathcal{B}$efore Relicario (Reli) joined my herd, the Paso Fino gelding had been in and out of two trial homes. Neither of those homes worked out, primarily because of Reli's unpredictable, erratic behavior. It was his reactivity that prompted Reli's owner to hire me a few months earlier. She needed to sell the horse but was at a loss in addressing his issues.

After my first few sessions with Reli I could not, in good faith, endorse him as a riding horse. Reli's trust issues were deep. I also sensed he might be experiencing some physical pain even though his owner said he had been deemed sound by a veterinarian. At the time, it was impossible to accurately assess the source of his physical discomfort because his general emotional reactivity was off the charts. He didn't want to be touched anywhere. It would take time to unravel all the factors that contributed to Reli's reactivity. Rebuilding his trust was the first step, and that step was a doozy.

In the end, the source of Reli's physical discomfort turned out to be instability and dysfunction in his **stifle joints**.

Worried about Reli's well-being on multiple levels, I used my network in the horse community to help his owner find a

A Stifle Joint is a complex joint in the hind limbs of quadruped mammals such as dogs and horses. It is the equivalent to the human knee.

permanent non-riding home for him. Paso Finos are a popular breed so I knew there would be interest. But Pasos are valued largely for their unique gait, which makes a riders' experience exceptionally smooth. If he couldn't be ridden, who would want him?

I made it clear upfront to everyone who inquired that Reli was not currently suitable for riding, and might never be. He was so reactive and untrusting, he had to be sedated for hoof trimming. He required a very experienced handler in most situations. Finding the right home for him was not going to be easy, especially in an industry where the majority of buyers are looking for an easy-going, "bomb-proof" riding partner.

Only one person showed serious interest in giving the unrideable 9-year-old Paso Fino (who could easily live 20 more years) a permanent home. This person was very interested in providing Reli a loving home but had nowhere to keep him except by himself in her backyard. Sending this horse to live alone, even when I knew he would be well-loved and cared for, was not a viable option. Reli was only settled and content when he was with his herd mates.

As I continued to search for the perfect "soft landing" for Reli, I continued to work on trust-building. The progress was slow, but he quickly stole my heart. Underneath his explosive exterior, Reli was a sensitive and sweet horse. He was simply screaming to be seen and heard. I sensed that Reli would do well in my liberty-based equine experiential learning program where the focus was on freedom, choice, and learning to nurture voluntary, mutual relationships. I mentioned the possibility to his owner. She was delighted and offered to sell him to me for one dollar, a symbolic transaction that would make the transfer of ownership official. She also graciously volunteered to sponsor the cost of his care for the first year he was with me.

After finalizing the paperwork, we made arrangements to pick up Reli with my horse trailer the following week. But there was something important I didn't know.

Reli had already decided he would never voluntarily get in another trailer. His experiences being trailered to trial homes (and back again) had given him every reason not to trust a human's motivation for transporting him. As soon as I started leading him toward my parked trailer, I saw a look of defiant determination settle in Reli's eye. His resistant energy was palpable. Before we even got to the trailer, I knew it would take a great deal of persuading to convince him to consider loading up.

I immediately slowed down, focused on my breathing, softened my body, and took care not to make Reli feel pressured. This horse was a ticking time bomb when distressed. His owner and I reassured him, hoping he could feel our loving intention. We explained that if he could trust us one more time, things would be different. Unfortunately, Reli was out of trust. Or at least that's how it seemed on the surface.

After three hours of patient and positive reinforcement with little progress, I seriously considered giving up for the day. The last thing I wanted to do was traumatize Reli further by physically forcing him onto the trailer. At the same time, I didn't want to leave him behind. Something in my gut was telling me I would regret that decision even more. Unsure what to do, I took Reli on a little walk. I asked him what it would take for him to trust me enough to get on the trailer. He stopped and stood perfectly still, looking at me with his piercing brown eye.

"I trust only myself."

I didn't so much hear Reli's words as feel the rawness behind them. His message was loud and clear. I let it sink in. I realized it didn't matter what I chose to do next. Reli didn't trust our intentions and nothing was going to change that. So I did the only thing I could do. I followed Reli's lead and trusted myself. I knew the sooner I could get Reli to my farm, the better it would be for everyone involved. I never like using pressure to force a horse onto a trailer, but I was grateful for Reli's clarity. It takes two willing partners to build trust and Reli wasn't interested.

When Reli and I returned to the trailer, his owner suggested we fashion a pulley system to push the horse in from behind, using a rope around his haunches. Given the situation, I agreed this would be the quickest, safest, and least traumatic approach to forcing Reli on the trailer. As soon as he assessed the situation for himself and realized the choice had been made for him, Reli ceded to the pressure and hopped in. Despite the fact that my new horse was anxious and stressed, pawing at the trailer floor, peace washed over me as I secured the doors and quickly headed for home.

That day didn't go the way I had hoped it would, but Reli and I made it home safely, and the courageous little horse didn't have to betray himself in the process. This experience completely transformed my perceptions around trust. As I drove Reli home, I knew in my heart that I would always be able to trust him in the most important way of all. He would be true to himself. Reli had witnessed me honoring my truth, too.

Reli continues to teach me what trust really means. He's helped me understand that building trust isn't just a two-way street. Our trust-building has been a crossroads where four critical paths intersect:

My ability to trust myself.
Reli's ability to trust himself.
My willingness to trust Reli.
Reli's willingness to trust me.

For Reli, trusting himself means listening to his gut and honoring what his lived experiences have taught him. I deeply respect the courage he shows in saying "no" to things that feel wrong to him. For me, trusting myself means knowing when I'm doing things for the right reasons, or admitting it if I'm not. When Reli wouldn't get on the trailer, he wasn't rejecting me or saying I was untrustworthy. He simply wasn't able or willing to offer his trust in a situation that terrified him (for good reason). He had chosen to trust others over himself previously, and regretted those decisions.

Horses never lie about how they feel. Deceit runs counter to the way they live and operate in the world. With only a rudimentary spoken language, horses rely largely on energy exchange and sensory perception to communicate and understand one another. As prey animals, horses excel at reading the nuances of energy and intention in others. To be deceived by a predator has deadly consequences. To intentionally deceive one's trusted (and trusting) herd mates could have equally deadly consequences. Understanding what's real and what isn't is of the utmost importance to horses who have none of our human motivations (or tolerance) for deceit. Horses need to know they can trust one another implicitly.

Meanwhile, words make it easy for humans to say one thing while feeling, acting, or behaving to the contrary. We've nurtured a uniquely human culture where pretending is a normal and accepted way of being. Fake it until you make it. Put up a good face. Never let 'em see you sweat. Be polite. A culture based in even the smallest deceit has ramifications. Humans often struggle to know where we stand with one another. We are also prone to deceiving ourselves into trusting others even when our gut tells us we shouldn't.

Horse wisdom reminds us:

- Trusting oneself means embracing the truth of our own experiences.
- Honesty is at the center of the crossroads of trust.
- Deceit is never innocuous.
- Breaches of trust change how we view ourselves and others.

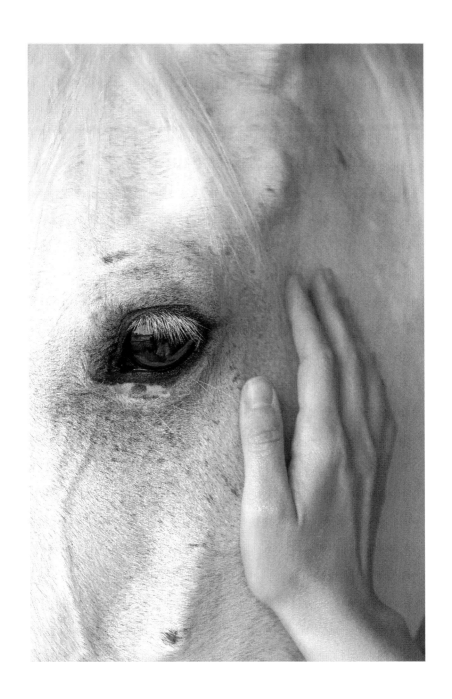

LESSON FIVE

Human Intelligence is Neither Superior nor Inferior

When testing for intelligence in animals, scientists hone in on specific abilities, such as problem-solving, communication, and self-awareness. Although humans have known for centuries that horses are highly trainable, equines were never considered smart enough to warrant significant scientific study of their intelligence— until recently. With each new study that's published, the evidence is mounting. Horses are among the most intelligent of animals, even by human standards. But who are we to stand judge and jury on the subject of intelligence?

Humans operate on the assumption that our species represents the most intelligent life form on Earth. However, there are many types of intelligence and not all are quantifiable. My personal experience living with horses leads me to believe the equine species is far more talented than the human species when it comes to embracing evolutionary intelligence.

Earlier this year, I observed a maiden mare and her newborn colt for the first few hours after birth. It was incredible to see how the mother and her son leaned into their innate evolutionary intelligence by following their instincts, even as they learned together in real time, experientially.

Within minutes of giving birth, the mother instinctively explored and licked her foal's face, gently removing any remnants of placenta from around his nose and mouth. Whether she consciously knew it or not, she was preparing him to suckle. During his first fifteen minutes of life, the colt took in the sights, sounds, smells, and feelings of being outside his mother's womb. Her constant presence, soft nickering, and loving touch grounded and comforted him. Within thirty minutes, he was fully focused on the monumental task of activating his long, wobbly legs. Meanwhile, mom followed her heart, knowing when to issue soft sounds of encouragement. She was attentive, with a strong protective presence, but never once did she micromanage his efforts. She understood that it was the colt's responsibility to do his part and call on his evolutionary intelligence. The mare patiently allowed her son to accomplish each step in his own way and time. Together they embraced the precious opportunities for rest, recovery, and connection between tries.

Once the colt was solidly on his feet and mobile, they meandered together away from the spot where the placenta and birth fluids covered the ground. Although this mare never lived in the wild, she knew that predators are attracted to the scent of birth. Neither the mare nor the foal second-guessed their inner urges and instincts. They didn't look to the other horses in the herd to tell them what to do. Meanwhile, those other horses were leaning into their evolutionary intelligence, too. Despite the fact that births are rare in this herd, all the horses understood that mother and son needed time alone to imprint on one another, solidifying the life-sustaining connection that began with conception. The mother-child bond not only increases a newborn's chances of survival, it's a sacred evolutionary safeguard that supports the long-term survival of the species.

With the foal's legs wobbling and unsteady, the next big hurdle was suckling. I marveled at how much of the responsibility fell to the baby. As a maiden at mothering (and likely quite uncomfortable physically in her milk-swollen teats), the mare seemed more concerned with keeping her baby in front of her, where she could easily keep track of him. It was the colt's strong instincts that drove him to nurse. He was determined to explore the underside of his mother's body. How did he know where to look? His lips and nose hunted for clues. As mother and son struggled to make sense of what happened next, there were many failed attempts. With each mistake, they learned together. And in between, they rested. Together.

It was so hard to resist my urge to step in and be "helpful." After all, I *knew* what needed to happen! And, I hated the anxiety riddling my body. I'd read that foals are born without infection-fighting antibodies in their blood. My scholarly intelligence warned me that this little colt needed to consume the colostrum in his mother's milk within the first few hours of life in order to receive the antibodies that would protect him from bacteria and viruses in the environment. My intuition kept me from interfering. "Let nature take its course," my evolutionary intelligence whispered. Wild mares and foals have figured out how to nurse for centuries. These two would, too.

I took a deep breath, cleared my thoughts, and focused on being present. I gave myself permission to relinquish responsibility and invite curiosity. I watched as this colt, only hours old, with no one showing him what to do, stayed committed to his quest to nurse. He didn't waiver or question his instincts. There was life-giving nourishment nearby, and he knew he would find it. Before long, the mare seemed less anxious and more comfortable with the colt moving around her. She no longer stressed when his clunky explorations took him behind her and temporarily out of sight and reach.

Although the colt hadn't tasted his mother's milk, the scent emanating from her swollen, waxy udder drew him in. The two horses fumbled their way into position. The colt leaned against his mother's side for balance as he finally latched onto her teat. The sound of his enthusiastic suckling brought tears to my eyes and joy to my heart! This new mare mother looked relieved, too. Every fiber of her being recognized that what was happening was right as rain.

Throughout this process, I thought about human mothers and babies, and their capacity to learn and know together in the same organic, intuitive way. The mare and her colt showed me what it means to cultivate and call on our evolutionary intelligence. They also modeled the art of collaborative experiential learning.

With every failed attempt, both horses gained "street smarts." They practiced trust and experienced vulnerability together. They listened to each other and their inner-knowing. They experimented. They encouraged each other. They took breaks together. They rested when they needed to. Most importantly, they never gave up. They never seemed frustrated or deflated. The pair stayed committed to each other and to the process. With each new effort, they built on what was working and abandoned what wasn't.

Few humans think about the innate intelligence that's passed down through the ages, but we should. Our preoccupation with intellectual learning and our obsessive drive to prepare in advance or control outcomes has caused us to bypass our inner guidance systems. When humans rely solely on medical professionals, standard protocols, and best practices, what do mothers and infants miss out on? What is the opportunity-cost of prioritizing scholarly expertise?

"Book smarts" is a purely human form of intelligence gained through reading and research. "Street smarts" develops as a result of real-world experience, including learning from our mistakes. It applies to all species. "Emotional intelligence" is the ability to navigate interpersonal relationships. Horses and other communal animals have high levels of emotional intelligence. "Intuition" is a natural ability to know something without proof or evidence. This gut feeling is our brain taking in sights, sounds, smells, and tastes from our environment and processing the information unconsciously, and providing a "feeling." Each of these types of intelligence is grounded and guided by instinct— the deep biological wisdom passed down from our ancestors.

A core aspect of both intellectual and embodied intelligence is learning: the acquisition or enhancement of knowledge or skills through experience, observation, awareness, reflection, repetition, and/or practical application. Horse and human brains evolved to learn in similar ways, but our motivations for learning differ.

When there is a clear, practical application for gaining knowledge, horses are highly motivated to learn. At some point, humans valued learning for learning's sake. Humans also measure intelligence based on the acquisition and recollection of information or the mastery of skills— even when there is no immediate practical application.

Formal education teaches skills that society tells us are valuable for our children's future. School is designed to enhance career success, a measure created by human society. The interpersonal skills that children learn while at school aren't the primary focus, yet these skills have life-long effects. Human educators are more concerned that the child can follow rules and directions, which sets them up to be good employees and to succeed according to human society's standards.

Colts and fillies don't go to school, take tests, do homework, or receive grades (until they're in human hands). For horses, most organic learning happens experientially, day-by-day, within the herd community. Equine education requires the practical application of embodied, integrated learning. This rich, herd-based experiential learning results in one of Earth's most socially intelligent species.

Think about the experience between the maiden mare and her colt as compared to the process that first-world human mothers navigate from childbirth to nursing.

Most expectant mothers read books in advance to prepare. Many engage in supplemental research, talk with their friends who are already mothers, and/or take classes to identify best practices, potential pitfalls, and tricks-of-the-trade. Our preoccupation with intellectual learning gives humans a clear advantage when it comes to being prepared, but preparatory-learning is a double-edged sword.

When humans enter into a situation with preconceived notions or judgments about how it should unfold, the less inclined they are to lean into evolutionary intelligence or innate wisdom. Knowing in advance all the things that could possibly go wrong also opens the door for debilitating anxiety and worry, neither of which the mother horse or her foal had felt.

Human infants are born helpless compared to horse babies. However, human mothers and infants are capable of learning and engaging collaboratively in the process of exploration. To nurse successfully, a human infant must be lifted and held close to his mother's chest. Could this be one of the reasons newborns instinctively cry at birth? A human mother, who hears the cry of her newborn infant, is compelled to pick up the infant and draw it to her chest to comfort, quiet, and protect it. These instinctual behaviors teach collaboration and support discovery of the logical next step.

There are many ways evolutionary intelligence could be applied in our human lives. Leaning into our innate curiosity about and connection with the natural world as a constant source of comfort, inspiration, connection, collaboration, and guidance engages our evolutionary intelligence.

Horse wisdom reminds us:

- All living beings have evolutionary intelligence.
- Embodied (experiential) learning, especially when it has a practical application, engages our evolutionary intelligence.
- Social and emotional intelligence can't be acquired or nurtured intellectually. It requires experiential learning.
- Intelligence includes everything we're born knowing plus everything (helpful or not) that we learn after.

༼∞༽

Beware the Privacy Dilemma

In horse herds, everything occurs in the open. In human society, privacy is prized. Horses around the world are masters at cultivating peaceful, harmonious communities. In fact, Mother Nature's model everywhere is one of balance and interdependent collaboration and co-existence. Meanwhile, humans perpetuate an almost constant state of conflict and turmoil. Cultivating greater harmony in the human realm requires tackling the privacy dilemma.

Modern humans have become obsessed with privacy. But privacy is a powerful portal to secrecy, which can become a mechanism for deceit with ill-intent. Trust is hard to nurture in a society where privacy is valued over transparency. Judgment plays into this dilemma as well. When hiding can prevent one from feeling judged, criticized, ostracized, or victimized, what's the motivation for being upfront and honest?

We deem privacy to be essential in all matters including medical records, personal finance, sexuality, religion, and politics. Of these, only sexuality exists in the natural world, and there's nothing private about it. In a wild horse herd, sexuality is expressed openly for all to witness and explore without judgment (although not without boundaries). Sexuality is the glue that holds equine society together! Reproduction and child-rearing drive herd organization, which is simple and highly effective. It's worth noting that humanity's more *civilized* approach to sexual privacy tends to be complicated and problematic.

When it comes to equine sexuality and reproduction, mares (female horses) run the show. The females are selective (in the wild) when deciding which stallion(s) they will allow to mate with them. Human control over equine sexuality and reproduction in the domestic world creates a wide array of emotional and behavioral issues in horses. Although not monogamous, horses exhibit a strong natural drive to form committed, long-term family groups called *natal bands* (sometimes referred to as harem bands). Natal bands typically have a single breeding stallion and one to ten mares. The stallion must work hard to earn the long-term loyalty of the mares who agree to enter into communal child-rearing with him. Stallions who have not been chosen (or perhaps don't care to be chosen) naturally organize into tight-knit *bachelor bands*.

Research shows that stallions who attract the largest number of loyal mares are the ones who prove themselves effective at raising healthy young to maturity. Good fathering skills as well as good diplomacy skills are essential. Nurturing strong relationships with the mares in his band is not enough. Successful breeding stallions also forge stable relations with the neighboring bachelors as well as the other natal band stallions in the herd's territory. A stallion's success as a father increases exponentially if he's good at avoiding unnecessary conflict. Mares are naturally wary of stallions whose behavior invites instability or chaos into the family unit.

Complete transparency empowers individual horses to manage their own sexuality and make wise reproductive choices. Relationship-building outside of the breeding season is a high priority for horses of both sexes. Mares and stallions who develop friendships will naturally stay in close proximity to one another, including when the mare comes into *season* (a regularly recurring state of sexual receptivity. In dogs, it is known as *heat*). If a stallion is offered and accepts breeding rights, he sticks very close to the mare throughout her seven days in season. During that time, the two will breed repeatedly, increasing her chances of conceiving.

There's little opportunity or motivation for non-consensual sex among horses. Male and female horses are similar in size and stature, which means mares are very capable of defending themselves against the unwanted advances of a rogue stallion. Chosen stallions are quite protective of their mates, but mares who live together will also join forces against a visiting stallion who acts too familiar without consent. This type of organic community policing happens quite naturally when every member is truthful and transparent. If a horse feels harassed, manipulated, or pressured (even by otherwise trusted herd mates), that horse makes it widely known by squealing, striking, kicking, or running away. The other members of the herd immediately pay attention and step in, if necessary, to diffuse the situation. By contrast, many human societies forbid sexual behavior in public spaces, making it easy for non-consensual activity to go undetected and unaddressed.

Interestingly, there are regions where natal bands of wild horses include more than one breeding stallion. In such cases, at breeding time (it's important to note that mares who live together tend to go into season at the same time), the band members voluntarily organize into two temporary sub-bands based on each mare's preference for breeding. When the mares are no longer actively in season, the band reunites and behaves as a cohesive family unit again. Researchers have documented instances where multiple stallions live in the same natal band but all the horses appear to have a mutual agreement that only one stallion will breed with the mares. These multi-stallion band scenarios have only been documented in regions where the rate of predation is extremely high, indicating that horses of both sexes cooperate creatively to nurture environments where young have the highest possible chance of survival.

Equine sexuality becomes much more convoluted when under human management. When I made the decision to breed my mare, Puck, I never thought to consider what Puck's feelings about this act might be or how she might approach decisions related to mating and motherhood. According to human protocols, I behaved responsibly when carefully selecting a stallion with a strong pedigree, excellent conformation, and a good track record of producing babies who go on to excel in the show ring. In human society, a *well-bred* horse is much less likely to end up neglected or discarded down the road. As Puck's owner and the breeder of her foal, my responsibilities were the only things I considered. Puck had no say in the selection of her *baby daddy*.

In fact, Puck never met the stallion who sired her only daughter. Much like many single mothers in human society, Puck found herself raising a child without the support of a robust and healthy herd family. My veterinarian artificially inseminated Puck using semen I purchased from the stallion's owner, which had been frozen and shipped to us from another state. There was absolutely no courtship, relationship-building, or choice involved. There was also no consent from either horse. The acts of collection and insemination were controlled by humans, managed independently, and conducted in private. These unnatural and contrived forms of sexual reproduction and manipulation would never exist (nor be tolerated) in the public domain of a healthy herd community.

Of all species on Earth, humans are the only species who made sexual behavior shameful and private. No other animals (or plants) are known to conceal or place judgment on sexuality. Sexuality is natural and at the heart of creating effective communities, particularly when communal child-rearing is necessary to prepare youngsters to become healthy, contributing adults.

Incest and in-breeding are almost non-existent among wild horses. Adults show little interest in breeding with youngsters they have raised communally. Likewise, siblings who grow up in the same natal band show little interest in breeding with one another. Once youngsters reach sexual maturity around two to three years of age, they naturally leave the natal band or get pushed out. Young adult females often get courted by neighboring bachelor stallions, and the young adult males either join an existing bachelor band or form a new one. The young stallions spend years forming deep, lifelong friendships, mentoring one another in the art of polite "mounting," sparring with one another (to develop effective fighting strategies), and nurturing other skills needed to become a natal band stallion, including how to co-exist peacefully with other stallions.

Horse wisdom reminds us:

- Privacy is not the panacea humanity makes it out to be.
- The privatization of sexuality (among other things) has many unintended consequences.
- Privacy doesn't exist in nature.
- The desire for privacy is exacerbated by ineffective boundaries and a lack of healthy interpersonal skills among members of a community.

Fear is a Fickle Friend

*H*orses have much to teach us about the art of embracing fear and staying in the present moment. A horse may graze or play with a companion, or even be trained or ridden by a human, while staying instinctively present and connected with the world around them. Horses actively engage in a constant state of receiving and categorizing sensory information. The equine brain and nervous system work together to divide sensory input into two primary categories:

Category A = normal/neutral/safe
Category B = unusual/suspect/unsafe

A few years ago, my neighbors set up a trampoline in their yard, not far from my back pasture. The horses paid little attention as the trampoline was assembled. They were aware of the activities, but weren't concerned. My neighbors on both sides regularly unload, assemble, and build contraptions in their yards. Children, grandchildren, nieces, and nephews of all ages frequently visit and play together outside, so the horses are very familiar with these sights and sounds. Typical neighborhood activities have been categorized as *normal/neutral/safe*. When familiar activities happen, the horses don't bother to lift their heads from grazing.

When the children climbed onto the fully assembled trampoline and started bouncing around, everything changed. The horses went on high alert. Two horses panicked and bolted away from the fence line. The other horses followed suit as if shot out of a cannon. Fear is one of life's most primal emotions, designed to motivate all species to take decisive action in order to stay alive. Horses have an intimate relationship with their sense of fear. They stand ready to embrace fear at a moment's notice. As flight animals, if horses can run away, they will. Fight is reserved as a last resort.

None of my horses had ever seen or heard children jumping on a trampoline. They had no context or category for the unfamiliar combination of sights and sounds emanating from the trampoline. For several days, the horses stayed clear of the fence line closest to the trampoline, even when no one was using it. When the children started jumping, laughing, and screaming in delight, the horses created more distance. After creating what they felt was a safe distance between themselves and the trampoline, the horses began to obsessively watch and listen.

Sometimes one or more of the horses got confident enough to tentatively move a little closer, get a better look, test the waters. Then, the horse returned to the others to confirm all was still well in the herd. Every fiber of their individual and collective beings sought to understand what they were seeing and hearing. The horses needed to be certain, without a shadow of a doubt, how this new activity should be categorized.

Watching my herd explore and manage their fears over the years has taught me a great deal about how to avoid long-term anxiety in my life. Horses never hesitate to embrace fear. They understand that fear is a friend. Fear has their best interest (survival) at heart! Fear only becomes problematic when it remains unresolved or turns into chronic anxiety. This is why horses do whatever it takes, for as long as it takes, to fully understand the things that cause them to feel fear. Horses dedicate their full attention to this life-saving process of investigation and will waste little time or energy on other pursuits until the work of categorizing is complete.

Humans do the opposite. We prefer to place our trust (often blindly) in other peoples' opinions or assurances rather than investigating our fears for ourselves. We rarely take the time to understand if, why, or when the things we fear actually pose an immediate or imminent threat to our safety or well-being. As a result, we obsess about our unresolved thoughts and emotions. Or we stuff our fears, creating toxic energy that gets stored in our bodies and creates *dis-ease*.

It took several days for all the horses in my herd to feel confident that the children playing, laughing, squealing, and intermittently jumping on the trampoline was normal/neutral. Most notably, the horses didn't all feel confident to the same extent at the same time. Some individuals took longer than others to return to their fully calm, relaxed, grazing patterns. Once the horses made their personal peace with the trampoline activity, they never showed concern about it again— until I introduced a new horse to my herd!

Reli had never experienced the sights and sounds of children jumping on a trampoline in any of his previous homes. Like the other horses, he panicked the first time he experienced it. But Reli had the benefit of the herd's collective confidence around these activities, which made his process of investigation and consideration a bit easier. While the other horses' lack of concern didn't immediately convince him that all was right in the world, their steady confidence did help him come to his own conclusion a little more quickly.

In the horse industry, equestrians often get frustrated when horses react out of fear, especially if the human knows (intellectually) that there's no immediate or actual danger. But feelings of fear should never be dismissed because unresolved fear becomes anxiety. Anxiety is one of the most dangerous and unpredictable energy forces on the planet. Pressuring horses to ignore or bury their fears is the easiest way to get injured—whether you're riding or standing near them. When a horse is nervous, it doesn't take much to trigger the full flight or fight response.

Unlike humans, horses don't hide their fears, nor are they compelled to calm down because their rider or handler tells them to, although most equestrians have tried. A horse's nervous system cannot regulate back to calm until his brain decides that everything is okay. The truth is that Humans can't either. Survival in the natural world requires meticulous attention to details and a categorical understanding of everything in one's environment. Missing details or miscategorizing a potential threat can have dire consequences.

Nothing gets a wild animal killed faster than failing to heed fear or misjudging a grave danger. At the same time, failing to resolve or understand a regular threat that is potentially manageable (such as a horse living in paranoia about being attacked by an alligator while drinking) can also be deadly.

Unresolved worry can keep a herd of wild horses from making their essential daily visit to the life-saving watering hole. Herd dehydration is far more deadly than the relatively small risk of an alligator attack. Horses are incredibly gifted at identifying patterns and noticing what happens *before what happens, happens.* In order for wild horses to successfully navigate fear, such as a potential alligator attack, they do the detailed work required to gain a profound understanding of alligator behavior.

Where do alligators hang out? From which direction do they most often attack? What times of day are they most and least active? At what depth can alligators stay submerged and hidden? How fast and far can an alligator travel over land? Are alligators more likely to attack when a horse is drinking by itself or when a group of horses are drinking together? By fully investigating the things they're concerned about, horses learn to navigate many situations that seem horribly precarious to us. In so doing, horses keep themselves and their herd mates relatively safe without falling victim to chronic anxiety.

Acute, intentional sensory presence allows horses (and humans if we so choose) to develop a robust familiarity with the sights, sounds, smells, tastes, textures, and even energies of our environment. Horses (vulnerable prey animals) model this instinctual process to nurture a deep sense of capability and safety.

Horse wisdom reminds us:

- Fear can be a lifesaving friend or a crippling enemy (if unresolved).
- Anxiety begs us to investigate the validity of our fears and develop effective mitigation strategies.
- Embracing our fears and trusting our instincts, including the natural drive to become curious when we feel safe, creates trust in our relationship with fear.
- Presence is a powerful tool for keeping fear and anxiety in check. Humans are often distracted, preoccupied, and not present.

LESSON EIGHT

Leadership is Meant to be Shared

*H*orses who trust and respect one another naturally engage in shared leadership within their herd communities. A healthy herd community honors seniority and values earned esteem. When hierarchical leadership is what best supports the safety, balance, and functionality of the herd community, horses embrace this form of leadership. However, hierarchical leadership is not the norm for horses. Equine organizational *charts* are intentionally flexible to ensure that the ultimate goal of maintaining a peaceful, balanced herd, and a unified sustainable community can be achieved and maintained.

Two years before Reli came to live with me, I introduced another new horse into my herd. Markus was a retired show horse whose career ended early due to chronic health conditions. Despite having only two previous owners, Markus was bounced between many different boarding facilities and show barns before eventually being sold to me for my equine-assisted learning program.

Prior to joining my herd, Markus spent most of his life living in various stalls and private paddocks. Like many domestic horses, he never had the opportunity to establish long-term friendships or be a member of a stable herd community.

After Markus arrived at my farm, it became clear he didn't understand how to participate in equine conversations around personal space or boundaries. He struggled to communicate effectively with the other horses and was often at a loss as to how he *should* behave. Worried about his safety, I initially put Markus with Shoki (the herd elder) to see how that would go. Markus' lack of social skills clearly made Shoki uneasy. The herd elder kept the newcomer at a distance by pinning his ears and lunging whenever Markus tried to approach. Thankfully, Markus—who had grown accustomed to being alone—was happy to stay on the periphery. There were no major scuffles until I tried adding the mares back into the mix.

Every time one or both of the mares showed an interest in interacting with Markus (or vice versa), Shoki aggressively chased Markus away, leaving the mares confused, anxious, and frustrated. All the horses had mixed feelings and none of the horses were on the same page!

Markus had no idea how to put Shoki at ease and the mares had no ability to control their natural hormonal responses. In the domestic horse industry, male horses not specifically used for breeding are typically castrated at a young age but female horses are left intact due to the high risk for medical complications. Every time I tried to put the herd together, things quickly devolved into chaos. In a desperate attempt to reclaim some sense of order in the herd, Shoki resorted to chasing Markus as far away as he could. Unfortunately, the fences prevented Markus from creating enough distance to put Shoki at ease. The newcomer instinctively ran for the corners (the farthest spot available to him) but inevitably found himself trapped with no way out. In order to escape, he'd have to jump the fence or run past Shoki.

At first, I was certain Markus would jump the fence. His size and talent for jumping would have made it easy. He froze instead. This behavior made no sense to Shoki. When turned out with a herd, most domestic horses learn *never to get caught in the corner*. Clearly Markus had missed that chapter of early learning. Shoki was determined to *school* him. The herd elder would whip around and start kicking out at Markus with both hind legs. This behavior carried an unmistakable message: get the heck out of there! But rather than run for it, Markus simply hunkered down and took the barrage of kicks. At that point, he was in no frame of mind to learn so I would run in and ask Shoki to back off so I could get Markus out of the corner. Thankfully, Shoki knew I was a trusted member of the herd and afforded me this grace.

Horses who grow up in a herd instinctively know that a cohesive community is imperative. A member who can't read body language and respond appropriately in a pinch makes the whole herd more vulnerable to strategically minded predators. Shoki wasn't kicking at Markus to hurt him. He was trying to teach a lesson that would stick.

Markus was far too anxious and stressed to make the connection. And, as a horse who didn't grow up in a herd, the language Shoki was speaking felt foreign to Markus. Overwhelmed and confused, Markus went into a state of learned helplessness, cringing even deeper into the corner. When a situation is believed to be beyond one's control, learned helplessness is a desperate coping strategy of the body and mind. I rushed to Markus' aid whenever I saw this scenario playing out. I didn't want him to get seriously injured! At the time, I was as dumbfounded (and frustrated) as Shoki about why Markus wasn't making the connection or doing more to protect himself. He was twice Shoki's size and could easily have barged past (or through) him.

A closer look at the lifestyle in which Markus was raised helped explain his behavior. In a busy barn environment, overstimulated or timid horses without the support of trusted herdmates, often learn to put their faces in the corner and tune out. In the context of barn living, corners are safe. If this coping strategy becomes ingrained, it can be hard to reprogram the brain. Whether horse or human, letting go of strategies that have served us in one circumstance, but which may not in another, is no easy task. In the face of unnatural or dysfunctional living conditions, it's easy to become dependent on unhealthy coping strategies.

Day after day, the no-win scenario between Markus and Shoki (with me playing guardian angel) kept repeating like an equine rendition of Groundhog Day. Neither horse was meeting the other *where he was*. I was on the verge of telling Markus' previous owner that the herd integration just wasn't going to work out. That's when Tempo stepped in with one of the most impressive acts of shared leadership I've ever witnessed.

Unbeknownst to the rest of us, Tempo had been watching things unfold and was carefully sizing up the situation. At only nine years old, Tempo was the youngest horse in the herd. She was raised by Shoki and Puck. She respected Shoki's seniority. In fact, I had never seen her question his decisions. After two weeks of watching this recurring standoff between the two geldings, Tempo decided it was time to intervene.

The next morning when Tempo sensed the tension rising again and before Shoki started to charge, she stepped in and positioned herself between the two geldings. With her head and tail held high, she arched her neck in an impressive display of self-assurance. Tempo used her body language to say, "I've got this."

At first, Shoki looked confused. But it only took a moment for the reality of the situation to set in. Tempo was not making a suggestion, or asking permission to lead. She was firmly taking the reins. I watched in amazement as Shoki willingly stepped back and passed the torch of shared leadership to his young protégé.

As it turns out, Tempo knew exactly what to do. When Shoki backed down, she turned around and charged at Markus herself, chasing him into the corner yet again. Just like Shoki, she spun around and kicked out at Markus with her hind feet. I was just about to run in and intervene when I noticed something was different. Unlike Shoki, Tempo wasn't actually kicking Markus. In fact, she was very intentionally maintaining a safe distance of several feet. I forced myself to wait and watch for a few more seconds. Then, I noticed a shift in Markus, too. He realized he wasn't being hurt. I saw his confusion, and so did Tempo. She turned and lunged in his direction, nipping strategically at his hind end. This caused Markus to take a step forward. A sense of relief washed over all of us. A flicker of hope and understanding flashed in Markus' eyes. Tempo didn't miss a beat. She pinned her ears and lunged toward Markus' tail. This time he scooted forward and found his path out of the corner.

Over the next few days, Tempo continued to monitor and manage the situation closely. Anytime Shoki felt the urge to go after Markus, she rushed in and took over. She must have repeated her far-more-empathetic version of the *corners lesson* at least a dozen times. Where Shoki managed to create frustration and despair, Tempo skillfully cultivated connection, understanding, and confidence. Before long, Markus began leaning into his own responsibility not to get trapped in a corner.

Once Markus was feeling confident enough to consistently navigate this scenario and protect his own personal space, Tempo humbly stepped into the background again. Shoki welcomed the now-much-more-herd-savvy Markus into the family, and peaceful cohabitation resumed.

There are many reasons why humans struggle to engage in the type of organic shared leadership that Shoki and Tempo demonstrated. Our organizational systems and community structures are often built on fixed chains of command, unnatural incentives and rewards, titles, credentials, policies, procedures, and strategic plans that promote rigidity and entitlement over collaboration and cooperative learning.

Horse wisdom reminds us:

- None of us are as smart as all of us.
- Diversity means there's always someone better equipped to see things differently.
- Untapped potential begs for opportunity.
- We are all meant to be leaders and followers, as well as students and teachers.

Success is Synonymous with Failure

The most meaningful "wins" in life are often born out of situations that initially feel like failures and/or appear to be tragedies. When my friend Billie passed away from cancer, I was devastated. It was her death that brought Shoki into my life, who taught me more about friendship than any human could have. Being friends with Shoki also helped me stay connected with Billie because I knew she was the only other person who would understand our horse/human bond. Similarly, it was Tempo's tragic bone cyst as a yearling that changed the course of both of our lives forever, opening doors I never dreamed possible. When I think about it, my entire personal journey with horses is one big example of how success is synonymous with failure.

Much to my chagrin, I didn't grow up in a family with horses. But my parents sent me to Camp Indian Echo, a Girl Scout sponsored program for horse-crazy girls that was run more like boot camp than summer camp. The Director was a tough, gruff, physically fit, middle-aged woman who went by the name Snakey. She greeted families in the parking lot upon arrival, immediately issuing a stern warning to the parents: "DO NOT help your daughter carry her personal gear down to the cabins. If she can't carry everything she packed by herself, in one load, the rest is going home with you!"

Snakey was my first introduction to the hardcore attitude that's so pervasive in the horse industry. *Making it* as an equestrian has less to do with one's compassion for horses and more to do with paying your dues, literally and figuratively. It's far easier to buy your way to success than to earn it. Decades of grunt work and proving your worth by riding mounts no one else wants (or dares to ride) might eventually earn you a modicum of respect, but those with financial means will always get access to the most-talented horses, best instructors, and most successful trainers. My only hope was to start at the bottom and work my way up. I distinctly remember being told by one of my early instructors that becoming a *good rider* would require falling off at least a hundred times. Then, she added, "and it's best if those falls are from at least one hundred different horses in one hundred different situations."

None of this phased me. My love for everything horse outweighed any amount of pain, discomfort, grunt-work, or sacrifice I might have to endure. Any illusion I had of *making it* as a competitive rider got shattered during my junior year in college. A freak riding accident left me with a broken neck and a fractured confidence. I was unfathomably lucky. After a six-month recovery, I walked away with no long-term physical complications. My body recovered fully, but the mental and emotional healing were more insidious.

Everyone at the barn (including my riding instructors) encouraged me to push through my fears and get back in the saddle as soon as I was able. I did my best to meet their expectations. I put up a strong front and exuded a fake outer confidence. Each time I mounted up for a lesson, my anxiety deepened. It was a matter of time until the next fall. During each ride, all I could think about was how much I wanted the lesson to end, so I could dismount before the inevitable happened. No matter how well a ride went, I couldn't shake the pervasive underlying fear. I focused on finding ways to never let my anxiety show. I still cherished my time at the barn and in the company of horses, but I started to feel like a fraud and a failure as an equestrian. No matter how hard I tried to fake it, there was no escaping the trauma I carried forward from my accident.

A few years later, I took a break from horses and assured myself that focusing on graduate school and building a traditional career was a good thing. Success would be much more likely (and much safer) if I sat in an office chair rather than atop a horse. It took many years for me to recognize that my fears around riding weren't a sign of failure. It was reality talking. In Lesson Four, we talked about trusting ourselves. My soul was begging to honor the truth my body had experienced. Riding a 1,000 pound prey animal is a very risky thing to do!

As it turned out, my inability to succeed (according to the "never show fear" mentality of the horse industry) wasn't failure at all. It was liberating because it set me on a path to discovering there are far more rewarding ways of sharing one's life with horses. Unfortunately, before I began to recognize and honor the gifts inherent in my perceived shortcomings, it took several more heart-wrenching failures and years of failed attempts to achieve success on other peoples' terms.

Opening my industry-conditioned mind and heart to alternative paths with horses wasn't easy. It's hard to imagine something you've never seen or experienced. As a child, I fantasized about galloping down the beach on a wild, black stallion, much like author Walter Farley's fictional character, Alec Ramsay. Fairy tales are wonderful but they can also spur us to believe impossible things are possible, such as hopping on a wild horse and riding like the wind without being hurt or afraid. Many *horse-crazy* kids hold onto these fantasies until something happens that shocks them back to reality. The truth is, gaining the riding and horsemanship skills required to achieve lofty goals on a horse's back require years of commitment—from the human and the horse. And the chances (for both) of getting seriously injured along the way are high.

It wasn't until Tempo came into my life, fifteen years after my college riding accident, that I started seriously considering a very important question. What is the horse getting out of our relationship? In Tempo's case, once she found herself confined to stall rest as a young horse and on the receiving end of daily oral medications, physical exams, and bi-weekly injections, she didn't feel she was getting anything worthwhile out of the relationship at all.

Her recovery protocol took away the two things that mattered most to her, and that matter most to many of us: freedom of choice and control over what is being done to our bodies. Tempo didn't care that everything I was doing was being done in the name of love and responsible caretaking to address the bone cyst and give her the best possible chance of a full recovery. She wasn't on-board with any of it.

Looking back now, I can't help but wonder what would have happened if I'd never read the *Black Stallion* series or seen images of Alec Ramsay and the Black galloping down the beach on the big screen. What if I hadn't been introduced to horses through the lens of a human-centric mindset? What if my early introduction to horses had been the opportunity to observe a peaceful horse herd and learn what's natural and enjoyable for their species? Would the thought of riding or training horses have occurred to me naturally? Would I have understood that horses are capable of taking care of themselves and one another? Might I have realized that horses have far more to teach humanity than we'll ever be able to teach them? And how might I have approached developing an organic friendship of equals with horses rather than being taught to use force and manipulation to achieve purely human goals?

Between the time of my riding accident and Tempo's message for me, I endured the roller coaster of many failed attempts to live up to the unrealistic pressures and expectations of the horse industry. In 1998, my friend Karen Zajicek and I co-founded the first statewide, non-profit equine rescue organization in South Carolina. I burned out within five years.

Equine rescue work opened my eyes to the horrific underbelly of the horse industry, including mind-boggling cases of neglect, a thriving but largely below-the-radar slaughter market, greed induced over-breeding, a hopelessly mismanaged Bureau of Land Management (BLM) mustang adoption program, the illegal use of horses as bait or training for dog-fighting, insufficient animal cruelty safeguards for horses in all sectors of the industry, and so much more. I went into rescue work knowing I could make a positive difference for horses in need and came out understanding it's impossible to use Band-aids to stop a hemorrhage. My failure to stomach the reality of equine rescue work taught me that the most responsible thing I could do within the human framework of ownership was provide a life-long, loving home for the horses in my care and model a different way of living in relationship with these amazing creatures.

I spent more than a decade studying and teaching the two primary methods of behavior modification used in horse training: positive reinforcement and negative reinforcement. It was only after both methods failed to help me resolve Tempo's aggressive behavior that I started to understand training a horse isn't the same as forging a healthy relationship with a horse. I'm a skilled trainer who could effectively manage most of Tempo's behaviors, most of the time, but despite my best efforts I was unable to extinguish the aggression until I stopped trying to train it out of her.

Tempo is a fiery and sensitive red-headed mare with a moral compass truer than any human I've ever met. My complicated and often heart-wrenching journey with Tempo led me to feel like a failure more times than I can count: failure as her caretaker, failure as her trainer, failure as her rider, and failure as her friend. In the end, she taught me what success actually entails—letting go of the things that aren't serving me (or those I love).

Through her living example, Tempo inspired me to leave a 17-year marriage that was deeply unhealthy for both me and my spouse. She showed me what it means to honor oneself, ask for what we need, and command the respect we deserve. Tempo reminded me that filling my own emotional cup should never require me to drain someone else's. She's the sole reason I found the courage to stop seeking success on other peoples' terms and start defining it for myself.

Tempo's aggression dissipated naturally once I stopped resenting it and started honoring the truth of it. Tempo yelled at me with her body language because I wasn't listening. *No* means *no*. When Tempo tells me she can't handle something, it means she can't handle it. She didn't need me to ask her to stuff her fears any more than stuffing mine helped me. Tempo needed me to honor how she was feeling. She needed me to step back and give her some space and time to collect herself. She needed me to allow her to take the lead so she could show me a way to approach things that felt better and safer to her. I established a deep pattern of disregarding Tempo's feelings in order to accomplish things I thought I needed to accomplish.

As it turns out, learning to release my attachment to the illusion that there's a *right way* to approach anything is the only true path to success and happiness.

Horses wisdom reminds us:

- The path of least resistance sometimes feels good for a reason.
- Frustration and failure motivate movement in a different direction.
- Success is a dangerous thing to define.
- If life feels like a constant struggle, it may be time to explore a different path.
- Endings beget new beginnings.
- Your failure may be a blessing in disguise.

∽∞⌀

Boundaries are Designed to be Flexible

$\mathcal{J}$ often sit on my front porch and watch the horses grazing. This is where I first noticed the graceful movements author Linda Kohanov described as the *boundary dance*. From my perspective, each horse appears to be enveloped in an invisible bubble of personal space. Guided by respect for these bubbles, the herd members gently shift and transform their positions in relation to one another but never lose their overall sense of cohesion and connection. Each horse moves independently, and yet one horse's choices inform, direct, and shift the others. Their movements impact one another and yet none seem to feel infringed upon. The longer I watch their graceful dance, the more aware I become that the space between beings is where authentic connection lives.

Horses are masters at modeling (and teaching) the art of flexible boundaries. Humans tend to think about boundaries as walls, but the image of bubbles enables us to imagine various levels of intimacy that don't require the absolute vulnerability of wide-open doors. Observing horses as they graze is akin to taking a graduate course in flexible, responsive boundaries, organic communication, and maintaining clear control of one's own experience. Rarely is there any hint of neediness, jealousy, or conflict in my herd. It's liberating to witness!

Do horses naturally know how to engage in this freedom-inducing boundary dance? And more importantly, can humans learn to dance like this in our herd communities?

Most humans embrace the need for boundaries only after we experience the consequences of not having any. Our first inclination when we feel violated or hurt by someone's words or actions is to build walls around our vulnerability. These walls are often the size of those surrounding Fort Knox. We want to be sure that the experience isn't repeated. When we think about boundaries from a false belief that erecting impenetrable walls is the best way to avoid being hurt, the idea of a graceful and flexible dance feels impossible. As with most things, the art of the boundary dance is easiest learned early in life rather than later.

A young horse begins to learn the art of the boundary dance when his mother grants permission for the other horses in the herd to interact with him. At first, Mom watches protectively, ready to intervene should any of the other horses blatantly disrespect the youngster's personal space or threaten his safety. Mother horses also serve as a safe haven whenever their foals feel insecure in their yet-under-developed communication skills and sense of self. However, if a youngster's over-inflated self-confidence or uninhibited curiosity leads him to disregard the boundaries of another horse, Mom intentionally stays out of the clarifying conversation.

A mother horse recognizes the importance of allowing other herd members to clarify their own boundaries. This early experiential learning teaches youngsters the most important thing there is to understand about boundaries; no individual can effectively or accurately represent or communicate the experience of any other individual. Consequences and responses are what teach young horses how to read the energy and intentions of others, when and how to adjust their choices accordingly, and eventually, how to effectively communicate their own boundaries in all situations.

Whenever domestic horse-keeping requires me to put my horses in a situation where there is a limited and valued resource, such as a single hay station, I get to witness what I have coined *the tenets of managing personal space* in action. It's physically impossible for all members in a herd of horses to access the hay station simultaneously without infringing upon another's personal space. This is when the fundamental rules of boundary setting get put into action:

1. Know thy personal space and how to communicate about it.
2. Own the boundary and mean it (i.e. be clear, committed, consistent and congruent in your communications around boundaries).
3. Never feel guilty for clarifying the space you need.
4. Don't judge yourself or others for personal space needs.
5. Boundary discussions are not about power and control. Never bully, micromanage, or go out of your way to punish those who attempt to understand and honor your needs. Walking away to create space is as effective as asking the other to move.

One day, I witnessed my herd elder, Shoki, napping under the run-in shelter by himself. His herd-mate, Markus, decided it would be nice to get out of the sun and join Shoki in the shade of the shelter. Prior to Markus joining the herd, he had little opportunity to learn the art of boundaries and failed to notice Shoki's body language. What should have been a very subtle point of negotiation became a much more animated conversation. Markus utterly failed to comprehend the message of Shoki's pinned ears. The message was, "That's close enough." As soon as Markus crossed the boundary line, Shoki lunged at him with bared teeth. Shoki knew he had to "own the boundary and mean it", and he did so without remorse.

Markus, who had missed the signals, had no trouble whatsoever understanding this clarified message. He quickly swerved out of the way, avoiding Shoki's teeth. That's when the interaction got interesting from my human perspective. Shoki didn't push Markus farther away. He didn't criticize, mock, or punish his friend for misunderstanding. Shoki also didn't feel compelled to apologize for yelling with his body language. In fact, Shoki didn't do or say anything more on the matter at all. He merely did what he needed to do in order to be understood. Period. Meanwhile, Markus didn't get defensive or yell back with his body language or stomp off in a huff of hurt feelings. After the exchange, Shoki calmly stepped back to his original napping spot and Markus respectfully settled into a spot of his own under the shelter that honored his desire to be there, and Shoki's clarified personal space. The end.

Humans who witness the more animated type of equine discussion that Shoki initiated (i.e. lunging with teeth bared) often project human judgments and worldview. For example, we might label the horse in Shoki's position as dominant and the horse in Markus' position as submissive. These two horses were not engaged in a power struggle. They committed to clarifying, in that moment, where each horse's personal space bubble began and ended.

After years of witnessing the way my horses openly embrace and nurture the nuanced art of the boundary dance, it became clear that humanity's reliance on external systems, rules, cultural expectations, peer pressure, and standards of etiquette interfere with our freedom to engage in organic negotiations and come to mutual understandings around personal space boundaries. A child pressured to hug someone may not feel naturally inclined to be that close to another person. He or she is being taught to disregard his or her feelings around personal space. A child required to share his toys (or face punishment) never has the opportunity to discover or decide for himself when playing with others feels intrinsically enjoyable.

Honoring personal space is the foundation upon which the boundary dance is built. Nothing brings horses more comfort, joy, and intrigue than playing with the eternal question, "Where do I end and you begin?" For horses, the boundary dance is not an extracurricular activity, hobby, or sport. It's an essential life skill that is practiced almost constantly. As with any dance, the more one practices, the more natural and fluid the dance becomes. Eventually, the boundary dance becomes second nature. In a well-established herd, the boundary dance can be so subtle that the energetic ripples are hardly noticeable. As humans looking in, all we see is the cohesive, graceful, seemingly coordinated movement of the community, which feels organic and incidental.

If horses who are not familiar with one another or are less skilled at communicating boundaries get thrown together, their dance can look choppy and uncoordinated. Movements may need to be exaggerated and responses can appear too strong or overdone. Rather than judge one another, the horses naturally engage in exploratory conversations using energy and intention to determine the edges of each individual's personal space. With horses, the end goal is always to reach a place of clarity and collective harmony.

Horse wisdom reminds us:

- We all need to see and be seen and understood.
- Boundaries define where I end and others begin.
- Clarity is far more powerful, and much more compassionate, than control.
- We should never cast judgment on someone for communicating clearly. Accurate information is critical when engaging in the boundary dance.
- Moving oneself is often easier, and more considerate, than asking another to move.

Communication is Not Optional

*H*umans are a highly verbal species. Our collective preoccupation with spoken and written language is a double-edged sword that can easily distract us from the deeper truth about communication. Because speaking and writing are both deliberate behaviors, we believe communication is an intentional act. Yet our bodies beg to differ. The moment life is conceived, highly effective communication starts happening at the cellular level—long before a fetus' brain is formed. Right now, as you read these words, the cells in your body received and responded to a wide array of complex information and stimuli, all without your conscious knowledge, control, or consent. To be alive is to automatically engage in a continuous, organic web of communication.

There was a specific moment when I became acutely aware that I was unintentionally communicating with the world around me. In the early morning, I got out of bed, walked to the bathroom, and flipped the light on. From the paddock, I heard Tempo respond with an enthusiastic nicker. The sound muffled through the walls but it seemed similar to her nicker of greeting when I walk out the door to feed the horses breakfast. I chuckled to myself, "I guess she knows I'm up!"

Prior to that morning, I never noticed the horses vocalizing in response to the bathroom light being turned on. Clearly Tempo had made the connection. The bathroom light is a precursor to breakfast being served. Horses are masters at noticing patterns so that part didn't surprise me. But the experience piqued my curiosity. I wondered what else the horses noticed and responded to that I wasn't aware of?

Tempo continued to greet the bathroom light with a nicker for the next three mornings. After confirming the cause-and-effect nature of the behavior, I tried an experiment. The next morning, I refrained from turning on the bathroom light when I got up and also stepped as quietly as possible when I walked across the room. I tried my best not to make any noise that might alert the horses I was up. And I thought I succeeded—until I turned on the water to brush my teeth. At that precise moment, I heard one of the horses blow out a big nostril-clearing release of air. This behavior can be the equine equivalent of letting out a huge sigh of relief. With a bit more experimentation, I confirmed that turning on the bathroom light first thing in the morning almost always elicits an enthusiastic nicker, but not always from the same horse. Any other indicator that I'm awake and moving (i.e. talking, toilet flushing, water faucets being turned on) is likely to prompt one or more sighs of relief and affirmation.

Initially I thought this connection between me and my horses was pretty remarkable. But is it really? It's been scientifically proven that horses have better hearing than humans. And as prey animals, they're hardwired to notice details. Every little change in the environment communicates valuable information to them. But why were the horses vocalizing in response to the realization that I was up? Why not just notice it in silence? Was one horse notifying the others that breakfast would soon be on the way? Why have a different vocal response to the bathroom light versus the water faucet? I was full of questions!

The more I thought about it, I started to wonder if the horses might be talking to me. They were letting me know that despite the darkness and the wall between us that they received the signals I sent them. There's no way to know the answer for sure but because horses are deeply communal animals, the vocalizations were intended to communicate information to someone. The pig, our resident crow family, countless other birds, squirrels, and many other forms of life are impacted in one way or another by my morning farm routine!

A few weeks later, I slept in. That's when my little research project got even more interesting! A sharp, piercing neigh snapped me out of my slumber. It was a much louder and more intense vocalization than the relatively soft "breakfast is coming" nicker or the "thank goodness she's up" sighing nose-blow. In fact, it sounded very similar to the urgent neigh my horses issue if one gets separated from the herd. My still-half-asleep brain processed this thought.

Then, I leapt out of bed and scrambled to the window to make sure all the horses were okay. As soon as Tempo saw me open the blinds, she nickered with relief as if to say, "Oh good! You're up!" Without a doubt, Tempo's clarion call was intended to get me moving. I looked at the clock and noted that she had generously let me sleep in for a full 30 minutes before sounding the alarm.

Thanks to the horses, I became aware that many other animals can easily see, hear, and/or sense what I'm doing inside the house. It's safe to assume that squirrels, lizards, snakes, birds, and other creatures living on my farm pay attention to my movements and patterns, too. I'm part of their environment, and whether I'm aware or not, I communicate information that's useful to them. They communicate a wealth of information that can be useful to me, too.

In an effort to better understand my ability to receive

sensory information beyond the walls of my house, I decided to stop turning on the television or radio during the day. I work from home so I wanted to notice what I could garner by paying attention. I was amazed! I can keep track of what's happening with the horses, pig, and many birds on my property as well as my neighbors' dogs, horses, and chickens. It is easy to recognize indicators of calmness, stress, confrontation, alarm, and playfulness. The diverse animal kingdom living outside my house is better than any alarm system at alerting me to unusual activity or unfamiliar visitors (human, avian, or animal) in the neighborhood.

When we allow ourselves to pay attention to what's going on in the larger environment around us, it's utterly impossible for any of us to engage in the activities of living without communicating valuable information to other living beings in the vicinity. Whether we choose to notice, respond, or engage with the information being offered is another matter. Based on my observations and experiences over the past few years, humans appear to be the only species who consistently ignores and disregards the majority of organic communication being offered by other species.

The natural world doesn't ignore what humans do, and we shouldn't ignore the natural world either. Animals and plants desperately try, often in vain, to get our attention or share important information with us. All I have to do is listen and maybe look out a window to confirm that "all is well" on my farm. The horses—and many other forms of life—provide instant feedback via their behavior, posture, appearance, movement, choices, and energy. Best of all, there is a high degree of confidence in the information they provide, because it's offered organically.

When I'm in the house, sometimes my horses go out of their

way to communicate something specific to me. One afternoon, I was completely engrossed in a writing project, typing away at my computer and noticed an uncommon sound in the back pasture. I was pretty sure it was the sound of a horse's hoof banging against the metal water trough. I'd heard this sound before and initially chalked it up to being incidental. Then, I heard it again. And again.

Before long, the repetitive tapping sound became irritating. I got up and looked out the kitchen window. As suspected, there was Tempo standing in front of the 100-gallon steel stock tank. She was staring straight at me. Then, she looked down into the tank and used her right front hoof to bang on the metal container. She banged twice in a row and looked back in my direction.

My brain struggled to make sense of what she was trying to communicate. "I know there's plenty of fresh water in there," I thought to myself. I scrubbed and partially refilled the tank earlier that morning. As I stood wondering, Tempo knocked her front hoof against the tank again and arched her neck to look even more deeply inside, but carefully avoided lowering her head to drink. Then, she looked in my direction again.

At this point, I felt highly motivated to go outside and investigate. When Tempo heard me open the front door, she whinnied in what felt like an enthusiastic, "Thank Goodness!" The mystery was solved as soon as I peered into the tank and saw a water-logged squirrel desperately trying to gain enough traction to clamber out. The little rodent was clearly close to exhaustion. I assumed he fell in while trying to steal a drink. Intentional or not, Tempo saved the squirrel's life. Perhaps she only wanted the unwelcome visitor removed from her trough, but the truth is, she could have done that for herself.

This incredible story of cross-species collaboration

demonstrates that effective communication and problem-solving don't require a shared verbal language. Wherever life exists, communication is inevitable and often happens organically.

Horse wisdom reminds us:

- Communication is constant.
- Communication can be conscious, unconscious, consensual, or non-consensual.
- The vast majority of communication is non-verbal.
- It's impossible to stop communicating.
- It takes intentional effort to notice information and communication coming from other beings.

LESSON TWELVE

❦

Human Language is Limiting

As a form of communication, human language is in its infancy. Our species' advanced capacity for complex verbal language sets us apart, but not always in constructive ways. When humans rely too heavily on verbal and written language, we limit our potential to thrive in the larger world. Human language has little currency beyond human society. Our preoccupation with verbal language also puts us at high-risk for incongruency, and in extreme cases, deception.

As an equine-assisted practitioner, my four-legged business partners don't speak English. They can't read or write, and yet I trust them explicitly. They are far more skilled than I am at seeing details and excel at grasping the bigger picture in almost any situation. Most importantly, they will always communicate honestly with me about how they feel, including:

- Their personal level of comfort with what's happening.
- Whether or not they feel up to participating.
- When and how they feel called or qualified to engage.
- What they see and understand that I may not.
- What kind of support or assistance they need from me.

- Whether or not they believe I'm on the right track (affirmation or redirection).
- What they sense or know to be true about a given person or situation.

I have yet to find a human partner who is as self-aware, honest, or forthright as my horses. Understanding what my horses are communicating requires listening with more than my ears. I use my eyes to notice their body language, observe their movements, and recognize patterns in their behavior. I use my awareness and intuition to feel the intention behind their actions. I tune into the shifting energies I feel. Horses expect us to be aware, notice, make connections, and tap into our shared history and context. When I succeed at staying present, rather than being distracted by my doubts, I receive intuitive messages that feel as organic as my own ideas. In return for my willingness to tap into these universal channels of communication, the horses collaborate as if they can read my mind. Nothing else I've ever experienced makes me feel more authentically connected and alive than interacting with my herd without the limitations and complications of human language!

That's not to say I never speak to my horses. I often vocalize sentiments such as "hello," "thank you," "how are you feeling" and "what do you think" out loud. Speaking these words means little to them, but it helps me embody the energy or intention I want to convey. The words are helpful to me, not them. Sometimes participants ask if the horses understand my words. "They understand the intention behind the words," I explain. Horses respond to everything, including our facial expressions, the tone of our voice, our demeanor, our heart rate and respiration, energy level, and body language. They don't care what we say, but pay attention to how we make them feel.

Context is one of the most important tools my horses use to communicate with me. Last year, one of my clients called to schedule an equine immersion experience, saying she needed to get out in nature and decompress. When she arrived for her session, she admitted to feeling preoccupied. She hoped the horses and I could support her in being more present and *getting out of her head*. We began with some sensory presence exercises to bring her awareness more into her body and help her feel more connected with the environment. Once she felt a little more settled, we entered the pasture to sit and observe the horses as they grazed. We kept our conversation simple and focused on what was happening with the horses.

After about 15 minutes, Markus approached, greeted the client with a friendly sniff, promptly dropped a big pile of manure in front of her chair, and walked off. We chuckled at his lack of inhibitions and strategically moved our chairs a few feet over. Not ten minutes later, Puck grazed her way behind us and dropped a manure pile of her own. This one landed a couple feet behind the client's chair.

"What's up with all the pooping?" she asked, rather wide-eyed. "I'm not sure," I admitted. "It's highly unusual for them to poop so close to where someone is sitting. Typically, horses will intentionally walk away from people to do their business." Part of my agreement with the horses is that I will always note a-typical behavior. Still, I had no idea what the horses might be trying to communicate. We shrugged it off and readjusted our chairs one more time. Within 5 minutes, Relicario came and joined us. He positioned himself a few feet to the right of the client's chair and looked like he was going to settle in for a rest. "How sweet," I mused, noting that the client must be making some progress in decompressing. At the time, Reli was the least confident around people of all the horses. He was obviously feeling safe and confident. We closed our eyes and leaned into the calm energy he offered. That's when we both heard the unmistakable "plop, plop" of horse manure hitting the ground. We looked at each other in disbelief. With our jaws still hanging open, we turned toward Reli to confirm that behind his hind legs was a steaming hot, fresh pile of manure. Upon seeing that we received his message, Reli sauntered off.

"Have your horses ever done anything like this before?" the client asked. "No," I said. "Never." It all felt very intentional. Then, the meaning of the message hit me like a ton of bricks. Without questioning where the thought came from I blurted out, "Do you have some crap you've been holding onto that you really need to let go of?"

The client burst into tears.

After regaining her composure, she said simply—and incredulously, "How did they know?" The client went on to explain that there was, indeed, some toxic stuff she'd been holding onto. This was precisely why she'd been so preoccupied when she arrived. "I know I need to let go of it. I've been trying for a long time. I just can't seem to move on from that painful experience." She went on to say that if the horses could feel the weight of what she was carrying, even as she sat there in the pasture, then she had to let it go. I could hear the decisiveness in her voice. It was already done. The horses had spoken.

Evolutionarily speaking, intuitive sensing and knowing is the oldest form of communication. Internal sensing existed long before the development of external sensory abilities. The earliest forms of life relied almost entirely on internal sensing and knowing. Most importantly, this essential ability has carried forward and remains present in all species living today, humans included. Intuition is the oldest and most universal language in all of life.

Any skill that is not practiced can be lost. Muscles that are not used atrophy. Horses put their intuition to use constantly, trusting their inner knowing to guide them as they navigate the often-complex and ever-shifting world around them. This is nature's way and has been for eons. We've conditioned ourselves to behave in opposition to nature's way. Not only do we focus our energy and intention on learning to use verbal and written language to communicate, but we also communicate primarily about one thing: our singularly human thoughts and beliefs.

The more we buy into the myth that cultivating our linguistic abilities is the ideal way to communicate the less attuned we become, as a species, to our natural intuitive ways to communicate. As we continue to isolate ourselves—individually and collectively—from the broader natural world, it becomes easier to convince ourselves that focusing on verbal and written language is *natural*. Most of us know, at least theoretically, that body language never lies. However, we convince ourselves to trust someone's words over what their body language and our intuitive knowing may be telling us.

Human infants, like all living beings, are born with the ability to feel and read energy-exchange. But rather than cultivate this ability, we systematically teach and condition our children to rely on the limitations of language instead. I often hear horse-people say that the reason they love spending time with horses is because horses never lie. It's not that horses have no reason or motivation to lie. They simply lack the tools for deceit. Over-reliance on verbal language to communicate makes lying, whether intentional or not, very easy. When we convince ourselves that words carry as much or more weight than intuition, energy exchange, behavior patterns, and body language, we reject our own innate intelligence.

As human societies become more globally connected through technology, it's easy to transmit written and verbal communication instantaneously over great distances. The addition of video-conferencing makes it possible to incorporate facial expressions and some limited aspects of body language into remote communications, but it's nowhere near the same as being together in person. Words make it easy to mislead and misinterpret. Of course, there are many instances when words can enhance communication, but this doesn't mean we should turn our back on more innate forms of communication available to us.

Horse wisdom reminds us:

- Human language is a gift to be handled with care and caution.
- Communication is intended to be a total body, experiential activity.
- When it comes to communication, context is paramount.
- When all we hear is someone's words, deceit is too easy.

First, Do No Harm

When it comes to caring for horses, there are many opinions about what is best in any given situation. The same is true for raising children or treating illness. Interestingly, the opinions of the individuals being cared for or treated (particularly when they are animals or children) are rarely taken into consideration when making decisions. If physicians and veterinarians took Hippocrates' words literally (i.e. "first, do no harm"), then Western Medicine would not exist. Surgery can't be conducted without doing harm to a patient's body. Pharmaceuticals come with a host of potentially harmful side effects. Even x-ray machines expose patients to potentially damaging radiation. Despite these known risks, doctors conduct tests, treat patients, and write prescriptions with the hope that their educated recommendations and treatment plans will ultimately help patients.

Robert H. Schmerling, MD, Senior Faculty Editor at Harvard Health Publishing suggests that, rather than taking "first, do no harm" literally, the phrase serves as a powerful reminder that doctors should neither overestimate their capacity to heal, nor underestimate their capacity to cause harm. This powerful reminder applies in a wide-range of contexts extending far beyond the field of medicine. We must learn to balance our personal desire and willingness to help in any given situation with an honest assessment of our potential to do more harm than good. For example, providing unconditional support to someone who isn't willing to help himself can create codependency. Stepping in to complete a task for an employee whose job (or safety!) depends on her ability to master the skills herself might make things easier or safer in the short term but cost the employee her job, health, or life in the long run. A new mother who feels embarrassed that she doesn't know how to handle a challenging situation with her child may avoid seeking help for fear of being judged or criticized, leaving the child to pay the ultimate price. Modern humans with the ability to see the big picture and make decisions accordingly are rare. Meanwhile, even the most domesticated horses remain naturally cognizant of the big picture, and their personal impact on it.

When I was a new equine-assisted learning practitioner, I felt compelled to plan in advance how each session would go. I took great care to map out specific activities and match each client with the horse I believed would be the best fit. The sessions went well so I had no reason to question the way I was doing things—until Tempo and Puck showed me how much I missed in regard to the bigger picture.

I decided in advance that I wanted to pair an incoming client with Puck. On her intake questionnaire, the client indicated a high level of fear around horses, so I wanted to start there and help her overcome that fear. Puck is the friendliest, calmest horse in my herd. I was confident she was the right horse for the job. However, once we started, I noticed that Puck was acting uncharacteristically stand-offish. I got the distinct feeling she didn't want to engage at all.

Interestingly, Puck's total disinterest allowed the client to start moving through her fear and hesitation, without me doing anything. Soon the woman became curious and eager to make a connection with Puck. I encouraged her to move closer to the mare. But every time the client took a step forward, Puck turned or moved away. Meanwhile, Tempo, who I had exiled to the adjoining paddock, was standing at the gate rattling the latch with her mouth. She indicated, in a very noisy way, that she wanted to come in. Prior to this session, Tempo had rarely shown interest in interacting with clients. She doesn't particularly like to be touched and is sensitive about allowing new people into her personal space. If Tempo doesn't like someone's energy, she has no qualms about pinning her ears or making threatening faces to say, "Back off!" I didn't want Tempo's assertive nature to worry or frighten this client.

Nothing seemed to be going according to my plan. "Why aren't the horses cooperating?" I thought. "This session is going to be a flop." Unsure what else to do, I directed the client to stand along the fence line behind me. I told her I was feeling the urge to open the gate and let the horses show us what they wanted to do. She was onboard, saying she too felt curious about why Tempo wanted to come in and why Puck was acting so aloof. As soon as I opened the gate, Tempo marched in. Puck made her exit almost as quickly.

My first thought was that I didn't want the client to get accidentally pinned against the fence if Tempo approached her directly, so I asked the woman to come back and join me at the center of the paddock. Tempo watched to see where we chose to stop. A moment later, the mare approached and deliberately positioned herself in front of the client. There was about three feet of space between their faces. The two stood looking at each other for a long time. I asked the client if she felt afraid. "Amazingly, no. I feel honored," she replied. Then, she asked, "Do you think Tempo will be okay if I touch her?"

"I honestly don't know. Tempo doesn't usually enjoy touch,

but she's surprised me more than once today," I replied. The client tentatively reached her hand forward. Tempo pinned her ears in response.

"That's a pretty clear no," I warned. Tempo taught me not to push the envelope when she says *no*. "Let's go back to the fence and stand in the shade while we give Tempo a minute. Maybe she'll show us in her own way why she wanted to come in here so badly."

When we got to the fence, I slipped out between two of the wooden rails so I could stand on the outside but still be available to intervene if need be. At that point, I let the client stay inside the enclosure alone with Tempo, who was showing no signs of being emotionally distressed or nervous. If I sensed Tempo's demeanor changing, I could duck back in immediately.

The client and I started chatting about how to read a horse's body language and why it's important to respect what they say, especially about their personal space. As we talked, Tempo slowly meandered into a position opposite the client. The mare had approached from one side and stopped with her body inches away from the client who found herself face-to-face with Tempo's shoulder. Tempo was very calm with an "ears forward" happy expression. It was a somewhat precarious position for the client and my brain wanted to move her to a safer place, but my gut told me not to.

"Maybe Tempo wants you to know that she's ready to accept your invitation to be touched, but only on her terms?" I suggested. I asked the client if she felt (energetically) that Tempo was inviting touch? "Yes, I sense that she's presenting me with the part of her body she is okay with having me touch." I explained that the wither (an area just above the shoulder) is a spot where horses sometimes mutually groom one another to nurture friendship. "Would you feel safe rubbing her gently on her wither to see how she responds?" I asked. The client nodded. She asked for a bit more guidance and followed my instructions to find the appropriate spot at the base of Tempo's neck. Tempo immediately relaxed into the woman's touch, lowered her head, and sighed.

My head was spinning. Not only was nothing going according to my plan but both mares were behaving in ways I'd never witnessed before. Still, I was elated that the client experienced such a gentle, voluntary interaction with a horse. I backed away from the fence to let them both enjoy the intimate connection for a few minutes. From my vantage point, all appeared to be well. The client was quiet as she continued to gently rub Tempo's wither. After a few minutes, I repositioned myself in order to see the client's face. It surprised me how tense and worried she looked.

"How are you doing?" I asked. "Honestly," the client replied, "I'm feeling trapped between Tempo and the fence. I don't have anywhere to move."

"You're not trapped," I reassured her. "You can leave any time you want."

"I don't know how to make her move out of the way. I'm scared."

"Where in the paddock would you rather be?" I asked. "Is there somewhere that feels safer in relation to Tempo?"

She nodded and pointed her head in the direction of the corner on the opposite side of the paddock. "Over there. But how can I get there? Tempo has me trapped!"

"You aren't trapped," I repeated. "Tempo's posture and demeanor both indicate she is here with you in friendship."

I encouraged the client to take a deep breath and focus on grounding herself, "Own the space you're inhabiting. Imagine that your feet extend down into the earth and your head extends up into the sky. Now, use your use hands, energy, and intention to communicate what you need Tempo to do. Lean into your feelings and desires, and gently ask Tempo to please step aside and give you the space you need to leave. Stay focused on the spot across the paddock where you want to go."

As soon as the client began to embody the intention she wanted rather than focusing on feeling trapped, Tempo sighed and took two steps to her right—creating plenty of space for the client to move out. "Good job!" I said encouragingly. "Now go to the spot you had in mind where you will feel safe."

Tempo and I both watched, without moving, as the woman walked to the opposite corner, took hold of the fence rail and bowed her head. Tempo let out another big sigh and promptly exited the paddock to join Puck. She seemed to say, "My job here is done." The client lifted her head, watched Tempo leave, and turned to me with a look of amazement. Tears were streaming down her face.

"Are you okay?" I asked. She nodded. "That was incredible." Her voice cracked with emotion and wonder. "I've felt trapped my whole life, and never once did it occur to me that all I had to do was ask for the space I needed. The other person would probably be happy to accommodate me!"

That's when it hit me: the horses knew far better than I did what this client needed to experience. She didn't need me to keep her safe. The client needed to know that she has the power within herself to ask for what she needs in order to feel safe. There wasn't a predetermined activity I could possibly have facilitated that would have come close to being as impactful as what Tempo and Puck orchestrated on their own. How did they both know exactly what was needed in this situation? I have no idea. Since that day, all the horses continue to demonstrate how clearly they see the bigger picture—even when I can't.

That was the last time I approached an equine-assisted learning session with a predetermined plan of action. Now, the horses and I work as a team in a much more organic way. I look for cues from them that I might be missing the bigger picture. They never let me down.

The lessons horses teach often include brief periods of mental and emotional discomfort as they gently push the edges of our human comfort zones. Horses understand that growth requires moving beyond our normal experiences. Does creating discomfort equate to doing harm? What if the discomfort is necessary in order to prevent greater harm in the long run? If I succeeded with my original plan, which was to prevent my client from feeling discomfort or fear around the horses, the unhealthy behavior pattern that was limiting her in so many areas of her life would have continued.

Both Puck and Tempo knew what the client needed to experience that day. They also knew what I needed to understand to become a more effective facilitator. Puck was not the *right* horse for the job that day, and yet, her role was instrumental. If I forced her to participate or viewed her lack of interest as being counter to my agenda, I would have missed the larger lesson about minding my own human limitations. "First, do no harm" is not as simple as it sounds.

Horse wisdom reminds us:

- It's essential to keep the big picture in mind.
- Other beings see and understand things we don't.
- It's important to acknowledge our limitations.
- Rather than going in knowing, practice the art of allowing.

LESSON FOURTEEN

Safety is Uncertain. Feeling Safe is Unequivocal

As prey animals, when horses feel threatened, they usually choose flight over fight. We think of flight as a mad dash in the opposite direction to the source of danger. However, research on the flight patterns of wild horses reveals that they don't just run away from danger; they very intentionally run toward a sense of safety. There's nothing chaotic about an equine stampede! Horses are fast, but an individual horse is not fast or strong enough to escape predators who hunt in packs or work in tandem to wear out their prey. Horses know the safest place to be when danger approaches is in the midst of a large cohesive herd.

To the uneducated eye, a stampede of horses may look like adrenaline-driven, blind madness but ethologist Lucy Rees explains there's a great deal of strategy involved. Horses instinctively employ a series of interconnected steps to mitigate danger, including:

- They avoid places where danger is known to lurk, frequenting places proven to be safe.
- Horses live in familiar herd communities where at least one vigilant member always acts as lookout while the others rest or sleep. The lookout

responsibility is voluntarily shared and rotates among members of the herd.

- Any horse who spots possible danger reacts with a commonly understood signal of alarm. *Alert* posture involves lifting their head and checking out their surroundings. *Alarm* posture has an ultra-high head, and body turned to face the object of concern with a rigid, tight, motionless body (much like a statue made of taught rubber bands, ready to explode).
- Herd members never question the alarm signal. They respond immediately with their full attention, cooperation, and cohesiveness by bunching together, ready to take flight at a moment's notice.
- Once in flight, the galloping horses remain closely bunched together. They're able to do this without colliding because they grow up practicing the art of synchronizing speed and direction with their playmates and mentors.
- A fleeing group of horses runs in the direction of the next nearest group of horses, if they can. In a stampede situation, the neighboring horses willingly join the stampede, creating greater protection and safety for all. The stampede continues to pick up additional groups of horses as they go, and continually running for as long as the threat is in imminent pursuit.
- At the end of a stampede, all the horses work together to reunite their original groupings.

Wild and domestic horses spend their days gaining an intimate knowledge of every path, inclination, nook, cranny, tree, bush, stone, and other obstacle in their home territories. Familiarity is what allows horses to safely bolt and run, even in poor visibility. If their access to other horses is restricted by fencing or there are no other horses nearby, they know the safest places to run toward.

A friend once told me the story of visiting a ranch where the farmer's herd of horses lived on a hundred acres, with free range to go wherever they wanted within their fenced territory. While she was there, they tacked up some of the horses to ride the perimeter (inside the enclosure) and check the fencing for needed repairs. The group split up, with three heading in one direction and the other three heading in the opposite direction. As my friend rode, she noticed that the land was riddled with gopher holes. She recalled being extremely anxious that one or more of the horses would step in a hole and get injured. She felt responsible for guiding her horse to avoid the holes.

When the two groups reunited at the halfway mark, the farmer suggested they take a gallop through the field on the way back. "But what about all the gopher holes?" my friend asked. She knew there was no way they could steer the horses safely through such a minefield at a gallop. "Don't worry," the farmer replied, "Just drop the reins and let the horses pick their own way. They live here. They know exactly where the holes are." And with that, he and his farm hand took off. Unconvinced, my friend and the other guests decided to hold their horses back and take it slow. Pretty soon their horses started jigging and dancing, getting more and more agitated the further away their herd mates ran.

Rather than fighting with their horses, my friend and her comrades decided to trust the farmer (and the horses) and let them gallop after their friends. She said it was the most terrifying ride of her life but somehow all the horses made it back safely without one instance of a horse accidentally stepping in a gopher hole. The farmer explained that horses have an incredible ability to map out every inch of their home territories. When they're out grazing and foraging, they're not just eating. They're busy exploring, investigating, and making mental notes. He said the horses know the pasture far better than he does, because that's where they live and inspect every inch. "Don't try something like that in a field where the horses aren't intimately familiar with the landscape though!"

In hindsight, after the stress of the moment had passed, my friend said it was one of the most liberating experiences to let go of her need to be in control and trust the horses to take the lead. After hearing that story, it became much easier for me to trust my horses to keep themselves safe. When making changes to their environment, I became more conscious of potential hazards and the importance of giving them time to investigate.

Within a familiar territory and in a trusted herd community, a horse feels safe grazing, playing, and sleeping. I often observe my horses resting or grazing in formations that ensure at least one member keeps watch in each direction. I've read that wild horses make efforts to know their predators preferred times of day and patterns for hunting, so the herd increases sentinel activity accordingly.

Like their ancestors, horses instinctively bunch together when they sense a potential threat. A lot of communal prey animals do this. Bunching makes it more difficult for potential predators to identify an individual target. As Rees explains, "Predators have a much more difficult time distinguishing their mark when scores of horse bodies are streaming past at high speed and suddenly merge together! The primary defense strategy of bunching in horses seems to be fusion and loss of identity." Research has shown that if an individual horse has to choose between running directly away from the source of danger alone, or running past the danger in order to reach and join other horses, the targeted horse will choose the latter. If a bonded group of horses is trapped, the herd will stick together and fight as a group.

Synchronizing is another key strategy horses employ against potential predators. Once imprinted, foals instinctively stick close to their mothers. Staying close to their mother is how the foal begins to learn the art of synchrony. Moving in synchrony is a skill horses practice daily, even when there is no immediate threat. Doing what other members of the herd do, moving together, and turning together is what keeps horses safe from collision in a stampede. Horses use synchrony as a primary tool for building cohesion and connection within the herd. The front runners in a stampede are often young adults because they tend to be the fastest. Being positioned in the front of a stampede does not mean you're leading the way. Instead, the front-running horses focus on synchronizing with the more seasoned majority of horses running behind them. It's typically the horses in the middle of a stampede who are making decisions about where to go next.

As Rees explains, "When observing a stampeding herd, you can see the center and rear horses change direction a fraction of a second before the front ones, who then shift to the right and turn, too. Synchrony is not a case of blindly following leaders but of doing what the majority are doing whether they are in front or behind." Sometimes a very young, elderly, injured, or sick horse who cannot keep up in a stampede will be left behind. When there is no other horse with which to synchronize, an isolated horse will often stop running. Domestic horses who get left behind or find themselves isolated are likely to panic or seek refuge with a lesser known companion (human or equine).

Some even find comfort joining up with a herd of cattle or other grazing animals.

Horses never voluntarily adopt an "each man for himself" mentality. Even in play, if one horse starts running, the others are likely to follow suit. As prey animals, horses are hard-wired to stick together! Communal play provides valuable opportunities to practice synchrony in motion. Colliding or tripping over one another in flight can mean certain death for horses that are being chased by predators.

With no ownership ties to, or sense of responsibility for, a particular place or possession, horses are willing to abandon their current location on a moment's notice in order to preserve or protect their lives. In human society, flight in the face of danger is often viewed as a weakness. This perspective is counter-intuitive given that our species lacks natural claws, teeth, horns, or hooves designed for fighting. Even as predators, humans evolved to have a healthy flight instinct, which is still evident in the way we startle and run from unexpected danger. Early *Homo sapiens* living a nomadic hunter-gatherer lifestyle found flight much more conducive to survival than fighting for their lives. Today's humans rely heavily on weapons, structures, doors, locks, fences, alarm systems, and law enforcement to keep us safe. In many ways, we are dissociating ourselves from our natural flight response rather than nurturing our version of stampede intelligence.

Much like horses, human beings are far more vulnerable when alone. In today's world, we frequently find ourselves feeling unsafe even in large groups. Why is this? When the others in a group are not trusted familiars or are seen as a potential threat, feelings of vulnerability tend to be stronger. Nurturing trust takes time and effort. Our isolationist tendencies, including adult children moving away from their family of origin, children and working professionals commuting to school or work, and constant travel outside our neighborhoods, result in communities that feel less familiar or safe. This lack of familiarity breeds feelings of vulnerability, suspicion, and mistrust. When situations of grave danger arise and the people we love and trust are not near, we lose our bearings and digress into panic and chaos. Humans who don't know one another are far more likely to clash, trample over one another, or collide.

Familiarity, trust, teamwork, and collaboration feed feelings of safety and preparedness. The more reliant we become on technology, weaponry, walls, and fences to make us feel safe, the more disconnected we become as a species from our own innate wisdom around survival and feelings of safety.

Horse wisdom reminds us:

- Familiarity helps us feel (and stay) safer.
- Trust (in ourselves and others) breeds a sense of safety.
- What we run toward is just as important as what we run from.
- We all feel safer when we're coping with danger together.

❧

Nature is the Source of Sanity

Spending every day outside with horses reminds us that humans shouldn't consider ourselves visitors in nature. The natural world is our home, too. Tending to horses reminds me how natural it is to rise with the sun and wrap up the day's activities before darkness falls. Sitting in the grass among the herd awakens a primal sense of connection to all life. Songbirds whistle their carefree songs, assuring me all is well. The sun warms my spirit and gentle breezes carry my worries away. A passing shadow may prompt me to look skyward where raptors silently ride the thermals on extended wings. Seeing their effortless flight patterns reminds me to go with the flow and keep a higher perspective in mind. In so many different ways, Mother Nature beckons our souls and welcomes us home with open arms. Unfortunately, we're often too distracted to notice nature's invitations. Humanity has abandoned our birthright, which is to live in harmony with all life. In doing so, we are also losing our connection to the ultimate source of sanity.

Like many children of the 1970's, I spent my childhood playing outdoors. Being outside brought me immense joy, but I never considered the natural world my home. Nor was I encouraged to think of nature in that way. Like the vast majority of modern humans, my family *visited* the beach, *picnicked* in the park, *vacationed* in the mountains, *hiked* on trails, and *camped* in the forest. The places we considered *home* were all manmade structures designed to separate us from the natural world. From inside the walls of my childhood home, I watched *Little House on the Prairie* and *Mutual of Omaha's Wild Kingdom* on television. These series captured my heart, but confirmed in my child's mind that humanity's proper place in relation to *the wild* is to separate ourselves from nature as much as possible.

The false belief that humanity is separate from nature allows us to consider the natural world with a sense of detached (and often irresponsible) curiosity. It also alienates us from our interdependence. As a child growing up in coastal Florida, I gleefully chased fiddler crabs with no concern for their experience and without recognition that my actions might be impacting the crabs' ability to feed themselves and their young during the precious hours when the tide was out. I enjoyed tossing our family's picnic scraps to seagulls on the beach without considering that I was conditioning the gulls to trust humans and crave foods that come wrapped in deadly plastics. I developed an utterly irrational fear of, and aversion to, cockroaches. This aversion still prompts me to grab the nearest hard object rather than marveling at the genius of their evolutionary design. My family taught me to be kind and compassionate to animals, which cannot override the pervasive and systemic human mindset of superiority.

The first time I looked directly into the depth of a horse's eye, I felt my soul reflected back to me. In that moment, nothing mattered except the calm, intense sense of recognition. It was as if the horse's soul and mine had known each other forever. Although I lacked the wisdom to make sense of the feelings, the experience awakened something primal within me. My intense emotional response was rationalized away by society as being a little girl's "infatuation with horses."

Today, I understand that my childhood experience of being dismissed as a "horse crazy kid" dissuaded me from exploring the deeper meaning behind my connection with horses. It isn't that horses are incredible beings. Within the context of the larger, interconnected, interdependent web of life on Earth, horses are no more (or less) incredible than any other species. Horses happen to be exceptional at awakening a sense of recognition in humans. This empowers them to serve as portals home to a source of sanity.

All forms of life have the potential to serve as portals to Mother Nature, the ultimate source of sanity. Even rock formations, streams, and glaciers can capture our amazement and remind us what alignment with the natural world feels like. However, horses are uniquely positioned to help humanity at this pivotal time. Horses are highly domesticated and have proven to be adaptable to living in captivity (even if captivity is not the lifestyle they would choose for themselves). The shared history between our two species means humans already understand horses as benevolent, peaceful, cooperative animals. Unlike dogs and cats, domesticated horses are far too big and messy to keep as pets living inside our homes. Horses require movement, large spaces, the companionship of other horses, a forage-based diet, and outdoor living to stay healthy. Our desire to interact and nurture meaningful relationships with horses gives humanity a compelling reason to step outside and spend significant amounts of time apart from our human-constructed world, priorities, and language.

The effectiveness of equine-assisted therapy in supporting the mental and emotional health of humans has spawned a great deal of interest and research. Studies conducted through the HeartMath Institute have proven that horses naturally have a *coherent* heart rate variability (HRV). This type of heart pattern indicates a system that can efficiently recover and adjust to stressful situations. A coherent HRV is a robust measure of well-being consistent with emotional states of calm and joy. When humans feel positive emotions, we exhibit this pattern, too. The electromagnetic field projected by a horse's heart is five times larger than that of a human, meaning when we stand near a horse we are being influenced by their electromagnetic field (imagine a sphere-shaped bubble that completely surrounds any human standing beside a horse). When we are inside this electromagnetic field, the horse's heart rhythm directly influences our heart rhythm. This partially explains the phenomenon reported by so many humans that we need only stand in the presence of a horse to feel an overwhelming sense of wellness and peace.

Studies continue to show that a wide array of people experience physiological benefits while interacting with horses, such as lowered blood pressure and heart rate, increased levels of beta-endorphins (neurotransmitters that serve as pain suppressors), decreased stress levels, reduced feelings of anger, hostility, tension, and anxiety, improved social functioning, and increased feelings of empowerment, trust, patience, and self-efficacy.

Horses stand ready to serve as bridges to reconnect more of humanity with the natural world. What might be possible when humanity intentionally embraces our individual and collective awareness that everything in nature has the potential to reconnect us with greater peace and sanity? The walls that divide us from the natural world are of our own making. We can dismantle them anytime we choose.

Horse wisdom reminds us:

- We may abandon our connection with nature, but nature will never abandon its connection with us.
- Presence with the outside world nurtures feelings of inner peace.
- There are many portals home to the source of sanity.
- We are never far from our true home.

LESSON SIXTEEN

∽◦◦∽

There is Dignity in Death

*E*very life has a beginning and an end. This universal truth applies to all living organisms from plants to animals and single-celled to complex life forms. Beginnings come in a variety of configurations: births, hatchings, sproutings, spawnings, and cell cycles. The common denominator is that birth represents the beginning of a temporary embodiment in physical form. Some physical forms, such as Mayflies, are designed to host life for only a few hours. Other physical forms, such as Oak trees, may host life for thousands of years.

Sooner or later, all physical forms deteriorate to the point of no longer sustaining life. We call this death. The death and decay of one physical form feeds and nourishes other physical forms. This self-perpetuating process creates a sustainable cycle of embodied life.

Death is every bit as essential as birth. The cycle of life requires both. The human species tries to deny that death is essential. Far too many people spend their whole lives trying to fend off the one thing that is unavoidable—death. Horses have shown me that accepting the truth about death is better than trying to deny, avoid, or delay death. When we honor the essential nature of death, we give it the dignity it deserves.

Shortly after purchasing my first horse, Lilith (Lili), we moved her from the boarding facility where she'd been living to our new farm a few hours away. Although I'd ridden horses most of my life, I'd never been responsible for the daily care of one. I didn't understand the importance of horses living with other horses. Lili was a calm horse by nature who happily traveled to shows and off-site trail rides; because of her demeanor, I mistakenly assumed the move to a new location wouldn't phase her. When Lilith arrived on my farm, she realized she was the only horse on the property. She became frantic, pacing the fence line, and anxiously calling out for her lost friends. Now and then, she stopped, stood alert, and listened longingly for familiar responses that never came.

For the first two days after her arrival, Lili barely ate or drank. I was unable to console her, which made me frantic, too. Worried that she would make herself sick, I decided to serve as a foster home for a horse in need who could serve as a companion to Lili. The rescue organization matched me with a horse named Andy who completed his mandatory quarantine period. When Andy arrived, I was stunned to see he was nothing more than skin and bones standing on four legs, covered in matted hair. It was hard to imagine the years of neglect he must have endured. My heart broke for Andy, but anger also boiled in my blood. Who could have done such a thing? Andy wasn't the least bit concerned. The moment he laid eyes on Lili, it was love at first sight.

Despite the years of neglect he endured, or quite possibly because of them, Andy bonded with Lili immediately. Within hours, my beloved mare was back to her old self, and Andy found a reason to live again. For almost a year, the two horses were inseparable. Wherever Lili went, Andy followed. With good care and proper nourishment, Andy's body filled out, and his coat shined like copper.

Then, one fateful afternoon tragedy struck. A bolt of

lightning struck a tree the two horses were standing under, sending a shockwave of electricity into the ground. The force of the electric bolt knocked both horses off their feet. Lili survived. Andy did not.

I expected Lili to become inconsolable as I was upon the death of her only companion, but she didn't. Shortly after getting knocked to the ground, Lili scrambled back to her feet. She regained her bearings and looked for Andy. Seeing his body lying on the ground, she walked over and intuitively knew that he was gone. She gently sniffed his face and neck and calmly walked a few yards away and returned to grazing. Our veterinarian confirmed that Andy had most likely died instantly.

Lili quietly mourned the loss of her companion but showed no obvious signs of distress. She seemed sullen for several weeks, as were we. It was most notable that Lili never called out for Andy, nor did she pace the fence or stop eating the way she had when I brought her home alone. Despite losing her beloved companion in a sudden tragic accident, Lili remained amazingly, calmly present—with herself and also with me.

The striking difference between Lili's emotional response to a herd mate dying versus her emotional response to being physically separated from living herd mates impacted me deeply. It was clear Lili understood that Andy had died and the others had not. Death innately made sense to her. Being separated from her living, breathing companions did not! I had no way of knowing whether Lilith had experienced the death of other horses, but not in the years I'd known her.

Twenty years have passed since Andy's death, and I've been present for the deaths of two other horses in my herd. In both cases, the remaining horses behaved in a similarly calm and accepting way, much like Lili. Every horse took time to acknowledge the deaths, each in their own unique way. The whole herd also came together after each death with profound reverence, respect, and grace. For portions of each day, the horses stood, individually and together, facing the burial spots. Their intentional quietness seemed meditative. They afforded themselves and one another plenty of time to sleep and rest.

After each death, I witnessed the intentional restructuring of roles within the herd as the remaining horses grappled to find a new balance. In what felt like a natural, collaborative tribute to the lives lost, each of the remaining horses took on aspects of the roles their lost comrade(s) had played. In this way, the losses also created opportunities for the living horses to nurture new skills and explore new dimensions of themselves. For example, when Shoki passed, Puck immediately stepped into a place of temporary leadership during the herd's mourning period, exhibiting an inner strength and resolve I'd never witnessed in her before. She became a powerful grounding force for the entire herd and for me as well. Shortly after Markus departed, Reli began showing up in a much more confident and interactive way for the equine-assisted learning sessions I facilitated. It wasn't that Puck and Reli behaved like their lost herdmates. They found the hidden resources within themselves that hadn't been needed before.

The members of my herd honored the burial places of both Shoki and Markus by walking a wide berth around the mounds for 4-6 months. After the loss of Markus, it took almost a year for the remaining three to settle into a new, balanced normal. This was most evident in their erratic sleep patterns and struggles to maintain a consistent resource-guarding hierarchy. If the horses had been members of a larger, more natural herd (especially one with a shared vision and purpose around communal child rearing), finding a new balance might have been easier. There's no question death impacts horses, but they also have a more enlightened and naturally healthy way of communally moving through death than humans. Most importantly, horses seem to understand that death is a sacred transition, and there's every bit as much dignity in the end of life as there is in the beginning.

Horse wisdom reminds us:

- Earthly bodies are but temporary vessels for the energy of life.
- Death sustains life and spurs transformational growth.
- Death is a powerful unifying force.
- A healthy relationship with death brings forth a healthy relationship with life.

LESSON SEVENTEEN

⚮

Healthy Community Begets Healthy Community

When it comes to nurturing healthy individuals, there is nothing more important than beginning with the end in mind: a healthy community. All living organisms are hardwired to adapt to the environment we're born into. Early learning sticks for a reason. It puts natural instincts into a meaningful context, enabling even the youngest of babies to begin making sense of a strange new world. Children rely on their parents, as well as other members of the community, to support them in developing effective life skills.

When a child is born into a healthy family and community, that child organically learns healthy ways of relating to others. If the family dynamics are dysfunctional, the child embodies coping strategies that are attuned to a dysfunctional environment. In codependent families, it's common for children to grow up believing their choices determine their parents' happiness. This early learning shapes how they choose partners and make decisions in their adult relationships. Children in unhealthy environments learn to seek temporary comfort to numb the pain of chronic stress through addictive behaviors, such as alcohol, shopping, junk food, and more. In families or communities where adults habitually disrespect children's physical, mental, or emotional space, the end result is young adults who have no awareness of their boundaries and little respect for the boundaries of others. Early learning experiences shape our core perceptions, beliefs, and patterns of behavior. This learning can override instinctual behaviors.

Last spring, a 70-year-old gentleman came to the farm for an equine immersion experience in celebration of his birthday. When he arrived, I asked what he hoped to get out of the session. "I'm frustrated," he responded. "Throughout my life, women have rejected my affection. I'm a loving, gregarious person. I like to express the love in my heart through hugs. When I'm enjoying someone's company, I reach out to touch them and make a connection. If we're getting along well, I might put my arm around them. I'm not inappropriate. I'm a respectful guy. Consistently, I get told my behavior is inappropriate or makes women uncomfortable. I'm tired of feeling rejected. Today, I want to spend time with a horse who will receive my love and affections without judgment."

"I'm sorry you've had the repeated experience of feeling rejected," I said. "It must be painful to not be able to express the love that's in your heart." He nodded. I went on to explain that I couldn't promise him the horses would be receptive to being touched. "They might be," I said. "But they just as easily might not be. I never force anything on the horses, so it will be completely up to them." As I finished my little speech, the man's attention shifted away from me to the pasture directly behind me. His face lit up with a smile. I turned around and saw that Puck was at the fence. My heart sang. Puck is very gregarious herself. She invites touch much more often than the other horses. Puck recognized a like-minded soul and was eager to give the gentleman what he'd come for!

We walked over to the fence and Puck sniffed the man's hand and nuzzled his face. Her actions were very respectful and gentle. Pure joy spread across the man's face as he received

Puck's affections. He stroked her face and neck in loving appreciation. The two continued interacting in this manner for several minutes. I was pleased he got the experience he wanted for his birthday. Then, he raised his arm and pointed to the pasture behind Puck. "I want to connect with that one!" he exclaimed enthusiastically.

Following his finger, I saw he was pointing to Tempo. I couldn't help chuckling to myself. Out loud I said, "You're unlikely to get your hands on that one. Tempo doesn't really like to be touched. She rarely gives visitors permission to pet her. You're better off enjoying your time here with Puck!"

The gentleman considered my words and responded matter-of-factly, "Tempo's the horse I'm most attracted to. I'm supposed to connect with her." I always try to honor other peoples' gut feelings as I honor my own. I strive to stay open to unforeseen possibilities. I quietly noted my internal concern that Tempo might reinforce the painful patterns in this man's life, so I focused on the possibility of facilitating a mutually respectful and safe connection between the two.

"Are you willing to connect with Tempo without touching her?" I asked. Puck had already shown him what it looks and feels like when a horse volunteers to be touched. I explained that Tempo had not made that same offer. When the man turned back to me, he looked deflated and defeated. "I'm willing but I don't have any idea how to connect with her without touching her."

"Don't worry," I reassured him, "there are other ways. The horses and I will show you." Hope sparkled in his eyes. A few minutes later, we entered the pasture. As soon as we closed the gate behind us, I drew the man's attention to Reli and Tempo. The two horses were grazing to our right, about 20 feet apart from each other. "What do you notice about the position of their bodies in relation to one another?" I asked.

"Both horses are facing away from us," he responded. "And their bodies are parallel."

"Yes, exactly. That means they're in alignment with one another, but not with us. Horses are always congruent, inside and out. Their bodies, minds, behavior, and choices are always aligned."

We stood watching for a few minutes. Reli and Tempo continued to graze side-by-side. They mirrored each other. When Tempo turned her head slightly to the right, Reli followed suit. When Reli took a step forward with his left front foot, so did Tempo. "This is so beautiful," I remarked. "Right now, Reli is demonstrating how he connects with Tempo. Do you see what's happening between them?"

When I pointed out the specific behaviors the man nodded. "Yes, I can see it."

"Would you like to try connecting with her in that way yourself?"

"Yes, very much! But I'm not sure how to do it."

I instructed the gentleman to watch as I approached the horses and modeled how to stand at a respectful distance, maintaining at least a full body-length of space between myself and Tempo in order to let her know I respected her boundaries. Then, I aligned my body with Tempo's shoulder, making sure the stance of my two legs were mirroring the positions of her front legs. When Tempo shifted her weight forward onto her left front foot, I shifted mine, too. When she took a step, I took a step. After a few minutes, I invited the gentleman to come stand beside me, on the opposite side from Tempo, so he could follow my lead and do what I was doing. Pretty soon, I could sense that my presence was no longer needed as a bridge. He and Tempo were in sync on their own.

"Will you be comfortable if I step away and let you continue on your own?"

He nodded affirmatively.

I walked away and found a comfortable spot to sit and observe. The mirroring game went on for quite some time. Both horse and human were completely absorbed. Wanting to check in, but not wanting to interrupt, I waited patiently for the gentleman to look up, hoping to catch his eye. He never took his eyes off Tempo. He appeared to be utterly entranced with the connection between them. After twenty more minutes, I made my way over and quietly stepped into alignment with them.

"It seems you're enjoying this," I said.

When he looked over and met my gaze, he was beaming. "This is the most amazing thing I've ever experienced!" he whispered. "Sometimes I'm taking the lead and sometimes she's taking the lead. It feels like we're dancing with each other, even from this distance. I could do this all day. I've never felt so connected!"

Later, when we were debriefing, the gentleman told me he will never take offense again if a woman isn't receptive to his hug. "Just because someone doesn't want to be touched doesn't mean they aren't interested in connecting with me. Tempo helped me understand this today. She truly wanted to connect with me, but on her terms. I could tell how much she enjoyed it and so did I! I'm glad I didn't get to touch her because if I had, I never would have understood what is possible without touch. Today was truly a gift for me."

This man spent his adult life feeling as though his genuine attempts to connect with women in a friendly way were being rejected. In less than an hour, Tempo taught him something no human had been able to help him understand. I don't know anything about the man's childhood, but I'm guessing his early learning experiences taught him that hugs are the best (or perhaps only) way to feel connected with another person. One thing's for certain, no one had taught him that connecting authentically isn't contingent on touch. Authentic connection requires seeing and being seen simultaneously.

Many humans struggle to feel in sync and at ease in our connections with other people. Most of us can recall times when we've been corrected, criticized, judged, or rejected for our attempts to connect. It's also not uncommon for a person—like this gentleman—to live a lifetime without ever knowing what it feels like to connect easily with others in an organic, healthy, respectful, consensual, and mutually enjoyable way.

Horses spend the vast majority of their time nurturing healthy relationships and healthy herd communities. This work is much more challenging for domestic horses than wild horses. Domestic horses face some of the same human-created obstacles that we struggle to cope with. For example, horses who grow up with their personal space consistently infringed upon by humans often have trouble understanding the concept of respecting personal space.

Humans choose to reside in houses with doors and walls that separate us (and our pets) from both the larger community and one another. Interestingly, we do the same to horses when we teach them to live in barns, stalls, and isolated paddocks. Humans choose to privatize property and punish others who trespass without permission. This makes spontaneous, organic interactions, and opportunities for unplanned connections rare. Interestingly, when we separate horses using fences or stall walls, we prevent them from having spontaneous, organic interactions, as well.

Humans choose to believe that personal preferences, behaviors, feelings, and beliefs should be private when in fact, these are the only circumstances that enable others to experience us for who we really are (and vice versa). We train horses to hide or stuff their honest preferences, behaviors, feelings, and choices as well—or face consequences including punishment.

One of the greatest advantages horses (whether wild or domestic) have over humans is that horses are only expected to be members of one herd community at a time. This enables horses to focus almost exclusively on cultivating healthy relationships in every moment they're together. Aside from the essential activities of eating and drinking, relationship building is paramount to horses. Meanwhile, humans put almost everything else, including our jobs and career goals, above relationship-building or creating community. We expect everyone to become productive, contributing members of multiple communities simultaneously—families, social groups, workplaces, professional organizations, school communities, sports teams, civic groups, political parties, church congregations, and the list goes on and on.

Life was never meant to be lived in the chaotic way we force ourselves to live. The human world is utterly unnatural, even for us. No other species expects its members to thrive while attempting to be contributing members of multiple communities at the same time. Humanity has become dysfunctionally addicted to our dysfunction, which is why spending time in a healthy horse herd can help us see our way out of our destructive cycle.

Horse wisdom reminds us:

- It's important for a community to begin with the end in mind—a healthy and balanced community.
- Human thinking alone cannot solve human created problems. We have a golden opportunity to look toward other species for healthier solutions to our communal problems.
- The natural world is a constant source of unadulterated higher wisdom.
- We are already members of the healthiest herd on Earth—the community of life.

Start with the End in Mind

Beginning with the end in mind requires a recognition that beginnings and endings are intimately intertwined. Starting this book helped you make it to the end. From here there are countless opportunities to go back, dig deeper, and apply what we've learned from the horses—individually and collectively. The *Horse Wisdom* journey brings us full circle, many times over. With each new experience, we uncover deeper layers begging to be explored. To support your continued journey, I've included questions to reflect upon and resources that I have found helpful for my journey. Take these reflections to your journal or use them as a way to guide a book club or saddle club discussions.

Lesson One: You're Free to Define Freedom for Yourself
- In what ways are humans currently living a life of captivity, literally or figuratively?
- What elements need to be in place for you to feel a sense of freedom in your daily life?
- Can you envision a world where the human species shares the same freedoms (and consequences) as the animal kingdom? What would that look like and how does this vision make you feel?

Lesson Two: Ownership is Unnatural
- In what ways do you feel owned by the things you own?
- What are some creative alternatives to traditional models of horse ownership that might be less oppressive to both horses and humans?
- What steps could you take to lessen the financial and emotional burdens of ownership?

- Do you think a world without ownership is possible? What are the primary obstacles humanity would need to overcome?

Lesson Three: Mind the Stories You Tell

- What stories and labels have defined or limited your life?
- Can you think of a time when your ego hijacked someone else's story (human or animals) and used the story for your purposes?
- Are there emotional wounds you carry that someone else understands? How might it be mutually beneficial to connect around your shared experience(s)?

Lesson Four: Trust Yourself First

- Can you think of a time when you failed to trust your instincts, feelings or inner-knowing?
- How might you handle a similar situation differently today?
- Why are breeches of trust (in ourselves or in relationship with others) so detrimental?
- What role (if any) should trust in a Higher Power (faith beyond self) play? Why?

Lesson Five: Human Intelligence is Neither Superior nor Inferior

- How connected do you feel with your evolutionary intelligence?
- What percentage of the things you've learned since birth have a meaningful practical application in your life today?

- What can you do to enhance your social and emotional intelligence?
- How might humans (as a species) reconnect with our evolutionary intelligence?

Lesson Six: Beware the Privacy Dilemma
- Is there a difference between personal space, alone time, and privacy? Explain the distinction as you see it.
- Is it possible to nurture and protect personal space and alone time in public? If so, how?
- What roles do space, distance, boundaries, and respect play in mitigating the perceived need for privacy?
- Choose an animal species to research or observe in the wild. How does that species nurture, honor, and respect personal space?

Lesson Seven: Fear is a Fickle Friend
- Can you think of a time (or more than one) when fear saved your life?
- What's one unresolved fear that causes you anxiety? How might you follow the horses' lead to investigate and re-categorize that fear?
- What would it look like if humans became diligent students of the thing(s) we fear?
- What can you do to move some of the things that cause you anxiety into the category of normal/ neutral/safe?

Lesson Eight: Leadership is Meant to be Shared

- Can you think of a time when you were encouraged to engage in shared leadership? How did the experience make you feel?
- Has your leadership potential ever gone unrecognized? How did that experience make you feel?
- Have you ever felt that leadership was your sole responsibility? What was that experience like for you?
- How can you nurture more opportunities for shared leadership in your family, workplace, and/or community activities?

Lesson Nine: Success is Synonymous with Failure

- Can you identify an experience in your life that initially felt like failure but turned out to be a fortunate twist of fate?
- How do you define success at this stage of your life?
- In what ways have various endings created new opportunities?
- Are you currently knocking your head against any walls that might indicate the opportunity to release attachment and explore different paths?

Lesson Ten: Boundaries are Designed to be Flexible

- Is a "yes" or "no" answer more helpful when trying to understand another person's boundaries? Why?
- Do you ever feel guilty for saying "no?" Are the feelings of guilt helpful? Why or why not?

- How often do you take it personally or feel upset when someone else says "no?" Why?
- When you envision boundaries as bubbles versus walls, how does it make you feel?

Lesson Eleven: Communication is not Optional
- List five things your family members (human or animal) regularly communicate to you unintentionally.
- What might you do to become more conscious of what and how you may be communicating?
- Take a 10 to 15 minute break to sit outside and notice the natural world. Make a list of indicators that tell you all is well. Do you notice any indicators of trouble or danger?
- As you go through your day, pay attention to what others are communicating non-verbally.

Lesson Twelve: Human Language is Limiting
- What are some examples of when your words (or someone else's) were taken out of context? What were the consequences?
- How can we tell when someone's words are incongruent with their body language, behavior, or choices? What role does our intuition play?
- What are some of the larger challenges humanity is facing that come as a result of relying too heavily on the words of others?
- Are there strategies that might help us pay greater attention to the larger context in more situations?

Lesson Thirteen: First, Do No Harm

- Have you ever had an experience when a plant or animal seemed to know or understand something on a deeper or more profound level than you did? Were you able to trust their knowing? Why or why not?
- Does the thought of higher intelligence in other species comfort you or frighten you? Why?
- Can you think of some examples in your life when you tried to help but ended up doing more harm than good? What did you learn about seeing and understanding the bigger picture?
- What are some opportunities you have in your current life to practice dropping your agenda to embrace the art of allowing?

Lesson Fourteen: Safety is Uncertain. Feeling Safe is Unequivocal.

- Is it possible to embrace and benefit from diversity while valuing familiarity at the same time? Does this become easier when we expand our conception of community beyond humans?
- What are some ways to nurture trust and feelings of safety even when we're with unfamiliar others? Can a focus on body language and energy exchange help facilitate this process?
- What sources of safety do you seek (literally or figuratively) when you feel scared?
- What are some strategies for nurturing togetherness despite physical distances? How can we (individually and collectively) build a stronger sense of cohesive community in our human lives?

Lesson Fifteen: Nature is the Source of Sanity

- How connected do you feel to nature in your daily life? What impact did your childhood experience have on your relationship with/to nature?
- What aspects of the natural world bring you the greatest sense of peace?
- Do you feel at home when you're in nature? Why or why not?
- What are three steps you can take to increase your connection with the natural world daily?

Lesson Sixteen: There is Dignity in Death

- Do you believe birth is more important/valuable than death? Why or why not?
- How often do you find yourself feeling anxious about death? What aspects of death worry or concern you the most? Would having more opportunities to experience death and talk about death as a natural and integral part of life help you feel less anxious about death?
- Which aspects of death tend to bring people closer together? Which aspects cause division and ill will? How can we do more (individually and collectively) to nurture the community-building aspects of death in order to enhance the experience of living for those who remain and remember?
- What are two steps you could take to enhance your comfort level in regard to death and dying, or to support others?

Lesson Seventeen: Healthy Community Begets Healthy Community

- When it comes to nurturing healthy communities, what does it mean to begin with the end in mind?
- When seeking solutions and answers in the face of today's biggest challenges, why do you think it's important for humanity to look beyond our species?
- What makes the natural world a source for trusted wisdom?
- What can you do to nurture a healthier community in your life?
- What steps can you take to nurture a greater sense of kinship with the larger community of life?

References & Resources

Here are some resources and sources of inspiration that have been most valuable on my journey. This list is by no means exhaustive, nor is any one resource (including this book) complete or perfect. Sample a bit from the sources that feel compelling to see what resonates for you:

The Horse Leads the Way: Honoring the True Role of the Horse in Equine Facilitated Practice by Angela Dunning

Animal Speak: The Spiritual & Magical Powers of Creatures Great & Small by Ted Andrews

The Business of Coaching with Horses by Schelli Whitehouse

Horses in Company by Lucy Rees

The Way of the Horse by Linda Kohanov

Boundaries and Protection by Pixie Lighthorse

Equine Leadership Magazine - equineleadership.ca

FreeHorse Arts - www.freehorsearts.org

Women Who Run with Horses podcast hosted by Hillary Schneider

Journey On podcast hosted by Warwick Schiller

Above all, continue to seek and create opportunities to spend time with horses on their terms. They have so much still to teach us!

May Horse Wisdom Be with You, always.

If you're interested in journeying on with me personally, check out these opportunities:

Virtual Horse Wisdom Book Club hosted on Patreon:
www.patreon.com/HorseWisdom

Blog – www.kimhallin.com
Facebook – www.facebook.com/Unbridled-LLC-with-Kim-Hallin-Connection-Healing-Growth-147527822543505
YouTube – www.youtube.com/KimHallin

If you visit Charleston, SC please reach out to schedule a customized equine immersion experience:
www.unbridled.guru

If you enjoyed this book, I hope you'll consider leaving a review and recommending it to others and gifting a copy to special friends and family members. **#shareitforward #buy2**

Request a signed copy through **www.kimhallin.com**.

References

Lesson 3: The BodyTalk System https://www.bodytalksystem.com/

Lesson 5: Jennifer Forsberg Meyer, "How Smart is Your Horse? Research studies on equine intelligence and behavior are bringing new insights into how smart horses really are." *Horse & Rider Magazine*, horseandrider.com, September 27, 2021

Lesson 6: *Horses in Company*, Lucy Rees, 2017, JA Allen, Ramsey, Marlborough Wiltshire, Chapter 6, pgs. 77-119

Lesson 9: *The Black Stallion* by Walter Farley, Random House Children's Books (Originally published in 1941)

Lesson 10: *Way of the Horse* by Linda Kohanov, 2007, New World Library, Novato, California, pg. 101

Lesson 13: Robert H. Schmerling, MD, Senior Faculty Editor, Harvard Health Publishing https://www.health.harvard.edu/blog/first-do-no-harm-201510138421

Lesson 14: *Horses in Company*, Lucy Rees, 2017, JA Allen, Ramsey, Marlborough Wiltshire, Chapter 4, pgs 48-65

Lesson 15: The HeartMath Institute, *Heart to Heart Communication with Horses*, Ann Baldwin, Ph.D. and Rollin McCraty, Ph.D., https://www.heartmath.org/resources/downloads/heart-heart-communication-horses/

Acknowledgments

This book would not have been possible without the inspired guidance of my book witch, Heather Dakota. Her compassionate approach to holding me accountable and willingness to push me beyond my comfort zone were instrumental. Thank you for convincing me to include the deeply personal stories that ultimately make the lessons so meaningful and accessible. I'm so grateful you said yes when I asked and for your skill in holding the sacred space required to bring this book to fruition.

I would never have started this book were it not for the ongoing encouragement and support of so many dear friends and mentors, most notably David Porter, Nancy Muñoz, Mary Segars, Skip and Skeet Godow, Dena Clair, and Jessica Austin Vides.

I'm blessed to have a loving partner in Chris Smith who lends his quiet, unwavering support to every endeavor I dream up.

I couldn't have survived this intensive year of writing and introspection had it not been for the financial and emotional support from the members of my Patreon Community and a few other special friends and extended-family members. You know who you are, and there are no words to convey my appreciation. I hope the book makes each and every one of you proud to have been a part of it.

Thank you to my mom, Carlyn Hallin Hastreiter, for recognizing and encouraging the writer in me from a young age and for modeling what it means to never give up.

Thank you to my dad, Dick Hallin, for supporting me every step of the way and honoring my often-messy journey of self discovery and actualization.

To my sister, Kirsten Strand, thank you for always walking beside me through thick and thin and for loving my equine family as deeply as you love our human family.

Thank you to Lili, Andy, Shoki, Puck, Tempo, Markus, Relicario, and Bartholomew the Pig for guiding me on this journey every day. And to the hundreds of participants who've spent time with us in the pasture practicing what it means to embrace the power of horse wisdom—you are inspiration and affirmation.

I also want to acknowledge the many other horse lovers who are bravely creating a movement away from the status quo and toward far more enlightened ways of believing, behaving, and partnering with the horses, one another, and ourselves. Our individual and collective efforts matter so much.

About the Author

Kim Hallin is the founder and equine-inspired soul guide at Unbridled, LLC in Charleston, South Carolina. As a compassionate horsewoman who upholds the integrity of the horse, Kim loves facilitating transformational healing experiences between humans and equines.

Kim nurtures a safe, supportive, and expansive learning environment that gently demystifies horse behavior while prompting humans to re-evaluate our choices, beliefs, and actions. While advocating for positive change in the horse industry, Kim recognizes the first step is unharnessing humanity from the limiting beliefs we place on ourselves. *Horse Wisdom: Life Lessons for Humanity* is her first book.

Learn more about Kim and her work at www.kimhallin.com

Made in United States
Orlando, FL
26 March 2022

16176014R00100